the *essential*
GUIDE TO
EMPLOYEE
ENGAGEMENT

the *essential* GUIDE TO EMPLOYEE ENGAGEMENT

Better business performance through staff satisfaction

Sarah Cook

London and Philadelphia

For Sylvia

Publisher's note
Every possible effort has been made to ensure that the information contained in this book is accurate at the time of going to press, and the publishers and authors cannot accept responsibility for any errors or omissions, however caused. No responsibility for loss or damage occasioned to any person acting, or refraining from action, as a result of the material in this publication can be accepted by the editor, the publisher or the author.

First published in Great Britain and the United States in 2008 by Kogan Page Limited
Reprinted 2009

120 Pentonville Road
London N1 9JN
United Kingdom
www.koganpage.com

525 South 4th Street, #241
Philadelphia PA 19147
USA

ISBN 978 0 7494 4944 5

British Library Cataloguing-in-Publication Data

A CIP record for this book is available from the British Library.

Library of Congress Cataloging-in-Publication Data

Cook, Sarah, 1955–
    The essential guide to employee engagement : better business performance through staff satisfaction / Sarah Cook.
        p. cm.
    ISBN 978–0–7494–4944–5
    1. Job satisfaction. 2. Personnel management. I. Title
    HF5549.5.j63c657 2008
    658.3'14--dc22
                        2008011170

Typeset by Saxon Graphics Ltd, Derby
Printed and bound in Great Britain by Bell & Bain Ltd, Glasgow

Contents

Preface

As global competition intensifies and organizations seek to attract and retain talent, 'engaging' employees becomes an issue of increasingly high importance. Business is now recognizing that 'engaged' employees are more productive, engender greater levels of customer satisfaction and loyalty, and are more likely to lead to organizational success.

However, in talking to managers across many different organizations, a series of questions emerged:

▌ What is employee engagement?

▌ What are the factors that drive employees to give of their best?

▌ Is employee engagement a passing fad or does it really improve organizational effectiveness?

▌ If employee engagement does work, how does a business 'engage' with its employees?

These are the key questions that have driven me to write this book.

This book is aimed at HR professionals, line managers and organizational change agents who want to increase the level of employee engagement in their organization. My intention in writing is to share not just what global best practice organizations do to engage their staff, but how they achieve this and profit from it, and what will stand in your way when you try to engage your employees. After the initial chapter, each chapter contains examples, key learning points and a checklist so that you can assess your organization and apply what you have learnt in a practical fashion.

Improving levels of employee engagement looks easy, but of course it isn't. Attempts to raise engagement levels are likely to founder unless there is a willingness and energy at a senior level in your business to take an holistic and long-term approach to building commitment to the organization.

There is no 'magic wand' that can be waved to bring about high levels of engagement and each business will need to address different factors. My intention is that the practical tools and techniques this book contains should help you raise the level of engagement in your organization, draw on best practice and ultimately bring about a healthy, more satisfied, customer-focused and innovative organization.

Sarah Cook
Stairway Consultancy Ltd
sarah@thestairway.co.uk

1

What is employee engagement?

As more and more businesses recognize that enthusiastic and committed employees add value to their organization not just in terms of productivity but also customer satisfaction, retention, profitability and long-term stakeholder value, 'employee engagement' is a much talked about issue at the highest levels in organizations today.

This initial chapter provides an explanation of what employee engagement is as well as outlining the benefits of employee engagement to the organization. It describes the rise of the 'engagement' phenomenon and whether this is a trend that is set to grow. The link between employee engagement and customer engagement is also discussed.

WHAT IS EMPLOYEE ENGAGEMENT?

In the course of one day recently I was made vividly aware of what employee engagement is all about. I had a day's leave and was catching up on small tasks that needed to be done at home and that I had left for some time to address. The first was to take my car in for a service. The second was to have a pair of glasses repaired, and the third on my list was to buy food for a dinner party that I was hosting that evening as a birthday celebration for a friend.

I started my day with a trip to the garage. I left my car for a routine service and agreed with the garage that they would call me that morning if extra work needed doing. Since I was due to be away the next day on a lengthy business trip where I needed my car, I was keen to get everything sorted out that day if possible.

Next, I called at the opticians – a high street chain that had recently been subject to a takeover and rebranding. I had bought a pair of glasses there that had broken three times. I was keen to get a replacement pair as none of the repairs the shop had made had solved the problem.

Finally, I stopped off at the supermarket to buy the food that I needed to prepare for the evening. The way that I was treated as a customer in each of these three interactions really brought home to me the power of employee engagement.

The person in the garage was polite and efficient. He went through the booking-in process and noted on the form my request to be called that morning if any other work needed to be done. The service provider called at 4.30 pm to tell me that the car was ready for collection. At this point he informed me of additional work that needed to be completed to make the car road worthy. He told me that they could do this work the next day. I expressed disappointment that he had not told me this before as it was late in the day to make alternative travel arrangements for the next day. The reply was that it was not the company's policy to call customers until the service work had been completed. The garage employee said, when I prompted, that he did not have a courtesy car available while the work was being completed, but he did give me the number of a local hire company so I could make arrangements to hire a car for myself the next day.

At the opticians my experience was worse. The person I dealt with was not receptive to my complaint. She refused to exchange the glasses or give me a refund, although she conceded that the damage was due to a manu-facturing fault. She blamed 'head office' for not being able to give a refund. She implied that I had somehow damaged the glasses and that I was at fault. The transaction ended in a stalemate with me threatening to contact the company's head office and the employee replying: 'Well go ahead then, what do I care?'

Exasperated, I moved on to the supermarket, where I bought the food for the dinner party, still stinging from the encounter with the unhelpful optician. On return home I began preparations for the evening celebration. On opening a carton of cream my mood turned even sourer when I discovered that the cream I had bought and that was an integral part of my recipe had gone off and I could not use it. I phoned the supermarket to complain as my day had gone from bad to worse. To my surprise the person on the other end of the phone was very receptive to my complaint.

He apologised profusely, took my details and offered to send me a full refund. Then, 15 minutes later, the doorbell rang. The person who I had spoken to on the telephone had arrived unexpectedly with two new replacement cartons of cream. He had taken responsibility for resolving my issue and gone out of his way to exceed my expectations.

In the course of one day as a customer I had encountered indifference, cynicism and unhelpfulness from two service providers and a positive, proactive approach from another. My 'cream story' became a talking point and certainly turned me into an advocate for the supermarket chain. The service I received from the garage was indifferent and did not make me want to go back. The experience at the optician retailer certainly made me an active detractor of that brand.

What has this to do with employee engagement?

A DEFINITION OF EMPLOYEE ENGAGEMENT

I am sure we can all recount similar stories of our experiences as customers. Yet just think what it would be like if the majority of your organization had employees who 'got the cream'.

Employee engagement is personified by the passion and energy employees have to give of their best to the organization to serve the customer. It is all about the willingness and ability of employees to give sustained discretionary effort to help their organization succeed.

Engagement is characterized by employees being committed to the organization, believing in what it stands for and being prepared to go above and beyond what is expected of them to deliver outstanding service to the customer. Employee engagement is more a psychological contract than a physical one. It is something the employee has to offer. As we will see, employees make a choice about how they behave and the extent to which they are engaged. Engaged employees feel inspired by their work, they are customer focused in their approach, they care about the future of the company and are prepared to invest their own effort to see that the organization succeeds.

Engagement can be summed up by how positively the employee:

▌ thinks about the organization;

▌ feels about the organization;

▌ is proactive in relation to achieving organizational goals for customers, colleagues and other stakeholders.

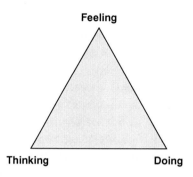

Figure 1.1 Three aspects of engagement

In other words, it is about the degree to which employees perform their role in a positive and proactive manner.

As Figure 1.1 shows, engagement therefore is about what employees think rationally about their employers, what they feel about them, their emotional connection, as well as what they do and say as a result in relation to their co-employees and their customers.

So why has employee engagement become so important across the globe? There are two key reasons: the increasing power of the customer and the increasing power of the employee.

THE POWER OF THE CUSTOMER

The customer now has much more choice of where to do business. Increasing competition, globalization, plus the power of the internet mean that customers' expectations have risen. We as customers now have much more discretionary power than previously. Furthermore, in today's busy society value for time is often as important as value for money. We are now more likely to take advice from our peer group on the internet as we are to wander from shop to shop seeking the best product. Businesses that will succeed in the future are those that make it easy for customers to do business with and that engage at an emotional level with the customer.

Effectively there are two costs a customer incurs in doing business with an organization: economical costs (time, effort, money, etc) and emotional costs (our feelings towards the brand, its products and employees, what it stands for, how we are treated, etc). In many cases we connect on an emotional basis with a brand. This emotion often overrides our logic. Witness makes of car or brands of clothing that become iconic.

Thinking about what we require from a service as a customer, effective customer interaction is a combination of an organization's ability to match the right products and services to the customer's needs – the what – and dealing with people in an effective and customer-centric manner – the how – as illustrated in Figure 1.2.

A poor product and poor person interaction leads potential customers to become cynics – actively telling others how bad a brand is. A good product but poor interaction with the sales person leads to indifference from the customer.

If the service provider deals with the customer well but the product or service does not meet their need, the customer will often give the organization a second chance. When an organization offers a good product and service and the interaction with the customer is exceptionally good, the customer becomes an advocate of the organization – an apostle.

As a customer we may have multiple interactions with service organizations. Service can be seen as a journey with numerous touch points for the customer. However, there are key 'moments of truth' in our interaction with service businesses that effectively make or break the impression we have of the organization. Service providers have an opportunity in how proactively they handle these situations to turn customers into apostles or cynics. My experience with the garage, the opticians and the supermarket is a good example of this. Where I have a choice, indifference or cynicism from the service provider is hardly likely to make me want to go back no matter how good the product or service is.

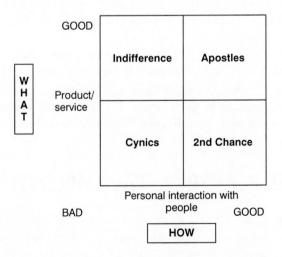

Figure 1.2   The what and the how of customer service

CUSTOMER EXPERIENCE

Today's best practice organizations recognize the power of the total customer experience in creating loyal customers. They appreciate that customers' purchase decisions are influenced by a number of factors. These are built up over a period of time and include:

▌ pre-purchase experiences such as external advertising, website, physical collateral and word of mouth;

▌ the purchase experience itself such as range of products and services offered, point of sale material, physical environment, product or service performance and delivery, interaction with the service provider;

▌ post-purchase experiences such as product or service quality, invoicing, service recovery, loyalty programmes.

Airline Virgin Atlantic, for example, recognizes the power of the total experience it provides its Upper Class customers. It places as much emphasis on the pre- and post-flight experience (offering chauffeur driven ride to the airport and from the flight to the customer's onward destination, having a customer clubhouse offering a range of services to customers, priority boarding, post-flight showers, etc).

Virgin Atlantic, like many other best practice organizations, nevertheless recognizes that the experience the customer has with the person who provides the service is key. Customers' perceptions of an organization are influenced above all by employees' willingness to help and provide responsive and prompt service, the empathy they demonstrate towards customers by showing a personal interest and the trust and confidence that they generate.

So employee behaviour is key to developing a long-term relationship with customers. The challenge today for organizations is to attract and engage customer-focused employees who are willing and able to step up to the challenge of the empowered customer. Employee engagement is key to ensuring that an organization is the one that wins the customer loyalty.

THE POWER OF THE EMPLOYEE

At the same time as the rise in the power of the customer, recent years have seen a remarkable shift in the world of work in mature market economies. It is now recognized that 'human capital' is a source of competitive advantage in many cases over and above technology and finance.

The traditional view of a 'job for life' has changed dramatically. Employees are now more likely to build a portfolio of skills and competencies that will help them develop multiple careers. At the same time the nature of jobs has changed. Organizations have downsized and delayered and this has meant doing more with less. The world of work is changing and there are an increasing number of employees who work part time or are on temporary contracts. Work is being increasingly being outsourced and 'off-shored'. Typical organizational structures are becoming more fluid with remote working and virtual teams becoming more common in organizations.

Likewise, management practices have shifted so that the old maxim: 'When an employee sells his labour, he sells his promise to obey commands' no longer holds true. The opening up of marketplaces, globalization, increased competition, the growing power of the consumer, technological advancement, pressure on margins and the demands of stakeholders have all contributed to a different employment environment from that known to our parents. Employees now have far more choice in where and how they work.

We have seen a shift in emphasis in employee relations from a 'community' approach such as via trade unions and collective bargaining, towards a focus on the individual relationship employees have with the organization. As employees' expectations of what they want from an employer increase, people with potential are more likely to move employment if they do not believe that they have the opportunity to develop. Increasing competition for talent has meant that employees now have more choice. Research has shown that in most organizations over a third of employees might leave or are planning to leave their organization.

The notion of job security and loyalty to one employer has been challenged by external market pressures and changing social norms. Previously managers could achieve results based on a command and control style of leadership which adopted a 'carrot and stick' approach to ensuring productivity and achieving results. Today the changing psychological contract has meant that organizations have had to find new ways to motivate their employees to encourage them to give of their best. Without guaranteed stability, employees are now looking for something else from their employers. In turn the employer is facing an increasing struggle to find ways to recruit and retain engaged employees.

In an era of global warming people at large have a better understanding of global issues. Today's workforce is more focused on aspects such as work–life balance and doing a meaningful job, making a difference for customers and the community it serves, not just shareholders.

In itself employee engagement isn't a radical departure from more enlightened management practices. The idea of creating a workforce that is happy, motivated and comprises people who want to and do give of their best makes logical, commercial sense.

What is important to the notion of employee engagement is the importance not just of creating a workforce that is satisfied and committed to the organization but one that strives to go the extra mile to offer discretionary effort to satisfy the customer. Thus the challenge for businesses today is not just on satisfying employees and getting them to stay with the organization but to create the environment where they want to and do give discretionary effort to go above and beyond what is written in their job description. Organizations therefore have to work harder to ensure that they win the loyalty of the best employees.

IS EMPLOYEE ENGAGEMENT A WESTERN PHENOMENON?

In the Western economy a growing trend is emerging for work–life balance and the need for meaningful work. People want to feel that they are making a difference and that what they do at work contributes to a better community and society This has fuelled the need for firms to take active steps to engage their workforce, but could the same be said for emerging economies?

India and Brazil have young and plentiful growing workforces; China has one of the world's largest but also oldest populations. The country's one child policy will mean that in the future as older workers retire there will be a labour shortage. All three countries are focused on manufacturing output. However, as efficiency and productivity increase analysts predict that these countries will need to start expanding into the service sector, investing in pharmaceuticals, telecom technology and research and development. Furthermore, these countries' domestic economies are set to advance and consumers' aspirations will continue rising.

Retention issues are already beginning to emerge in these countries, with workers quick to leave for better remuneration and higher job titles. Countries such as China and India are experiencing skills shortages in many fields. These countries' workforces frequently display an ambition and a desire to get ahead that contrasts with their US counterparts. Research by consultancy DDI shows that employees in China, for example, are more satisfied than their US counterparts with their work–life balance. They are more willing to make personal sacrifices, they have a stronger desire for promotion and find work more fulfilling than their personal life. Conversely, workers in China in the DDI study were twice less likely to agree with the statement 'I have too much to do' than their US counterparts.

So while US employees are striving for balance and are fairly cautious about making personal sacrifices to advance their careers, their Chinese counterparts have a thirst for advancement, new knowledge and skills.

I predict that employee engagement will become equally as important for emerging economies as it will for Western ones. This is because as economies develop and there is more choice of employment, organizations will find it increasing challenging to attract and retain talent and potential. Research currently shows that Chinese employees rate involvement and engagement as poor, and in a Towers Perrins' survey only 8 per cent of workers were actively engaged. In order to harness the ambition of workers in emerging economies businesses will need to put in place programmes for robust recruitment and selection, ongoing development and succession planning. Proctor & Gamble, for example, have been successful in attracting and retaining high-quality managers although the compensation package is not as attractive as elsewhere because they offer continuous learning and development to their managers. I foresee that businesses that thoroughly embrace the concept of employee engagement in emerging markets, motivating others and building trust, will carve a clear competitive advantage for themselves in the future. This is because as economies become less dependent on manufacturing markets and more focused on service industries, the importance of employees becoming ambassadors for the brand increases.

	China (%)	United States (%)
Satisfied with work–life balance	80	69
Willing to make personal sacrifices	93	66
Desire for promotion to senior level	75	65
Agree with the statement: 'Work is more fulfilling than my personal life'	45	3
Have too much work to do	23	49

Source: DDI Talent Management in Action report 2006–07

Figure 1.3   Retention issues

IDENTIFYING ACTIVELY ENGAGED EMPLOYEES

In the three examples I experienced in one day, it was clear which employee was engaged. Assuming I was correct and the supermarket employee was highly engaged, I would probably see this through:

- Cognitive engagement: the degree to which the employee focuses very hard on work. Engaged employees are focused and at one with their work. For example, they are not distracted from what they are doing, they display single-mindedness and high energy.

- Emotional engagement: the degree to which the employee feels engrossed in the work. Engaged employees are 'in the zone', they are engrossed in what they are doing to the extent that they do not become distracted. They live in the 'here and now' when they are at work.

- Physical engagement: the degree to which employees are willing to go the extra mile, not just in terms of customer service but also for themselves, for example in taking responsibility for their own learning and development, in finding new ways of doing things and in putting in discretionary effort.

- Advocacy: the extent to which employees recommend the organization to their family and friends in terms of job opportunities and doing business with the organization. A key determinant is how employees portray the organization to others when they are outside work. Do they show pride in the organization? Do they relate to it and talk as 'we' rather than 'they?'

There is a buzz about an organization where employees are truly engaged. People feel trusted, valued and empowered. They are emotionally committed and personally involved; there are high levels of motivation and enthusiasm.

One way of describing the level of engagement that an employee has is to gauge their enthusiasm and energy level and the degree of positivity that they display at work. The model has two dimensions. The first is employees' attitude towards the customer, their colleagues and the organization, be it positive or negative. The second is their enthusiasm and drive towards activity, be it positive (active) or negative (inactive).

The degree to which people demonstrate a positive attitude and their type and levels of activity can be translated into likely engagement patterns. Figure 1.4 illustrates simple behavioural patterns that can be seen in regard to engagement.

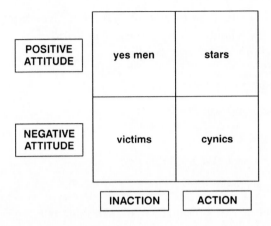

Figure 1.4   Engagement levels

Employees defined as 'stars' have a positive attitude to change and are action oriented. They have high energy, enthusiasm and make discretionary effort. They are realistic about obstacles they encounter and how to overcome them.

Stars are fully engaged with the organization. Their behaviour is characterized by:

▌ giving discretionary effort to serve the customer;

▌ seeing the silver lining hidden beneath the dark clouds;

▌ viewing change as a challenge and opportunity;

▌ treating life as a continuous learning experience;

▌ expanding their personal comfort zone.

Stars tend to:

▌ feel comfortable with the need for change;

▌ be open to possibilities and ideas;

▌ be optimistic about the long-term future;

▌ like to be challenged and stretched;

▌ be realists, not afraid of short-term mistakes or setbacks.

'Cynics' display a negative attitude and high levels of activity. This group are actively disengaged. They have a lot of energy and can be very vocal, but what they focus on is the negative – what is not working in the organization. They are keen to disassociate themselves from the organization and actively tell others why change won't work.

Cynics' behaviour is characterized by:

▋ always seeing the negatives;

▋ criticizing ideas and solutions;

▋ expressing frustration;

▋ focusing on the past: 'We tried this five years ago...'

▋ arguing against change;

▋ being oblivious to the consequences of their negativity;

▋ bringing other people such as the victims and yes men round to their perspective.

Cynics feel:

▋ in the right and angry at the world for ignoring them;

▋ frustrated when there is confusion and whingeing;

▋ not listened to, excluded, constrained;

▋ overtly confident in their own ability;

▋ rebellious, determined to block change they do not own;

▋ unsympathetic to the stress felt by others.

'Yes men' are characterized as neither actively engaged nor disengaged. They are the 'coasters', prepared to drift along, saying the right things but following things through with energy, passion or action.

Yes men are characterized by behaviour that is about:

▋ avoiding taking risks;

▋ keeping a low profile;

▋ trying to ride things out without drawing attention to themselves;

▋ acknowledging good ideas but being reluctant to change themselves.

Although Yes men may be positive about what is happening in an organization, they are reluctant to get involved. They feel threatened when too exposed and are comfortable to watch from the sidelines.

'Victims' can be described as having a negative attitude and lacking drive. This inactivity, coupled with their negative approach towards new ideas, leads to inertia. Although less vocal than cynics, they still are disengaged from the organization; everything is 'done to them', they do not take an active part in organizational life. However, unlike cynics they lack the energy or drive to vocalize this.

Victims react by:

▌ avoiding confronting issues;

▌ retreating into 'safety' – burying their heads in the sand;

▌ avoiding risk, doing the minimum;

▌ avoiding thinking about what might happen.

Victims may feel unhappy and/or depressed, overwhelmed by work, powerless and fearful of mistakes, but their lack of confidence means that they do not actively seek to find other employment or to improve their current working life.

Characteristic phrases which each type may use are shown in Figure 1.5.

It is clear from this model that stars are the people who exceed customers' expectations and deliver the 'wow factor'. They are advocates for the organization and are truly champions of the brand. These people help create a high degree of customer engagement with the brand. What do I mean by this? Customer engagement describes the health of the relationship between a customer and a brand. This relationship drives financial success. It can be characterized by how well the organization

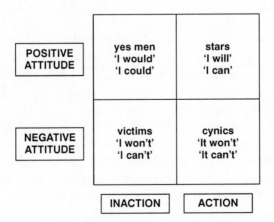

Figure 1.5 Characteristic phrases

delivers against its brand promise, to what extent it treats its customers fairly, and how well it deals with complaints and issues.

Research shows that customer apostles are five times as likely to remain loyal to the brand, they spend more with the organization, are more profitable as customers and promote the brand to other people.

Reichheld, who is a leading authority on customer retention and loyalty, has developed an 'ultimate question' which captures the degree to which customers are engaged with an organization. This is: How likely is it that you would recommend company X to a friend or colleague? Bain's 'Net Promoter Score' (www.netpromoter.com) system measures a company's rating by subtracting the ratio of detractors from that of promoters. This can be done by telephone or e-mail surveys or paper questionnaires. Bain's research shows that high NPS results invariably correlate with high growth. For example, he found at Dell and Asda that a 5 per cent increase in retention can yield up to 100 per cent increase in profits.

In many ways customer engagement is a product of employee engagement. The studies conducted by Gallup around employee engagement have consistently shown a connection between employee engagement and customer engagement.

Typically, highly engaged employees believe that they can positively impact the quality of their company's products and services as well as positively impacting the customer experience.

John Varley, Chief Executive Officer at Barclays Bank, is quoted as saying that employee engagement and customer centricity complement each other by 'causing people to ask themselves, "Why am I doing what I am doing, and what does it mean for the experience that our customers are having?"'

Uxbridge-based Rackspace Managed Hosting is an IT support company known for its approach to looking after staff and customers. It believes that the more aligned the motivations and objectives of individuals and their employer are, the more successful the organization will be. Therefore, rather than filling positions, it looks to recruit people who will fit the company's distinct culture and then finds roles for them. As Jacques Grayling, the UK managing director says: 'You can't teach someone attitude; it needs to be there from the beginning.'

Rackspace has grown by over 89 per cent a year over the past two years. Staff turnover is about 7 per cent. But its customer satisfaction score is the most telling indicator of its success. It uses the NPS system, which looks at whether customers would recommend you to someone else or not. Rackspace's NPS stands at nearly 80 per cent, compared with an average of 14 per cent across industry and commerce as a whole. Its CEO says: 'You don't get engaged customers without engaged employees.'

EMPLOYEE COMMITMENT AND SATISFACTION DOES NOT EQUATE TO ENGAGEMENT

Nowadays, like customer satisfaction most organizations measure employee satisfaction. So what is the difference is between employee engagement, commitment and satisfaction? A typical question many companies ask is: We measure employee satisfaction and loyalty already so what's new?

Employee engagement is closely aligned to the concept developed in the 1990s of the service-profit chain but there is a big difference and I will go on to explain this shortly.

First, let me outline the concept. The service-profit chain (or service-value chain as it is now called) is a model of organizational success that is based on research by Heskett, Sasser and Schlesinger of Harvard Business School. They demonstrated a clear link between what happens inside the organization and the quality of the service provided to the external customer. In their 1997 book the three Harvard professors show how leading service organizations grow and develop profitable businesses. They demonstrated a quantifiable set of relationships that link profit and growth not only to customer loyalty and satisfaction derived from good external service quality (how customers perceive the organization versus the competition) but also to high levels of employee loyalty and satisfaction which derive from good internal relationships and working environment (internal service quality).

Their theory, called the service-profit chain or service-value chain can be represented as shown in Figure 1.6.

The premise of the service-profit chain is that staff satisfaction = customer satisfaction. Stew Leonard, head of a well-known US dairy store, says: 'If you look after your staff, they will look after the customers who in turn will look after your profits.'

The connection between the behaviours of employees and an organization's bottom line was first recognized 15 years ago by US retail company Sears. By applying the principles of the service-profit chain, in a year its biggest loss-making division, Merchandising, went from a US $3 billion deficit to a net income of US $752 million. To explain the model I'll run through it link by link.

> Studies in Europe as well as in the United States show that in order to retain customers and maintain profitable growth, organizations need to ensure that they have a large number of advocates for their business.

▌ It is only truly 'delighted' customers who remain loyal to the organization. Customer satisfaction and delight is directly related to the experience customers receive wherever and whenever they contact the organization.

▌ The quality of external service delivery is a reflection of the quality of service that people in the organization provide each other.

▌ Employee retention and satisfaction are essential to this. In particular, when employees do not feel valued or appreciated, they are less likely to deliver excellent internal or external service.

▌ Therefore the style of leadership that is demonstrated across the business determines the quality of the service experience.

This philosophy suggests that internal customer satisfaction is equally as important as external customer satisfaction. This is because how different parts of an organization interact with their internal customers has a direct impact on employee satisfaction (in particular the degree to which they feel valued by the organization) and employee retention. This in turn influences external service quality, customer satisfaction and retention. Figure 1.7 illustrates the elements in creating profit and growth or value for the organization.

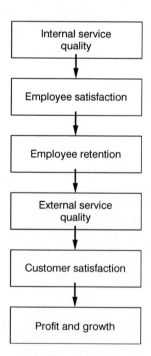

Figure 1.6   The service-profit chain

Business imperative	Internal service quality	Employee satisfaction/retention	Service value	Customer satisfaction/retention	Commercial success
Organizations need to have:	Elements that create good internal service are:	Elements that drive employee satisfaction and retention are:	Service value is visible through:	Customer retention is enhanced by:	Equates to:
customer-focused mission and goals	the right tools for the job	leaders who focus on the customer	clear customer promise	seamless service: management of the total customer experience	profit
strategies to address competition, global environment, global and local economy, technology, pace of change	adequate resources	leaders who role model excellent service	product features		shareholder value
	effective and efficient systems	clear direction setting (goals, service vision and customer promise)	consistency	listening and responding to customer needs and concerns	customer lifetime value – the longer the customer remains with the organization, the more profitable they become
	appropriate structure	open communication	reliability		
	appropriate job design	appropriate employee selection and development	quality	how the service is delivered	employee retention
	relevant core competencies	empowerment	value for money	service recovery strategies when things go wrong	reinvestment for the future
	effective internal measures	coaching	loyalty programmes		
		effective team building and management			
		reward and recognition			

Figure 1.7 Creating value, profit and growth

This model has been used by many organizations to develop and grow their businesses. As a consequence, there is a lot of empirical evidence that proves that there is a correlation between employee satisfaction measures and customer satisfaction measures. Let's look at some of the statistics.

▌ AT&T, for example, found that a 3 per cent increase in employee satisfaction related to a 1 per cent increase in customer satisfaction.

▌ US retailer Sears found a 10 per cent increase in employee satisfaction associated with a 2.5 per cent increase in customer satisfaction and a 1 per cent rise in sales.

▌ In the UK, the Nationwide Building Society has found similar links between HR practices, employee commitment and mortgage sales.

▌ Quick-service restaurant chain Taco Bell observed that the 20 per cent of stores with the highest employee retention rates enjoyed double the sales and 55 per cent higher profits than the 20 per cent of stores with the lowest employee retention rates.

There is often a time lag between the impact of an increase in employee satisfaction and the increase in customer satisfaction of 6–18 months, but the correlation is always there.

ENGAGEMENT VERSUS SATISFACTION AND LOYALTY

My concern with the concept of the service-profit chain is that employee loyalty and satisfaction does not necessarily mean that employees are engaged and offer discretionary effort.

Take, for example, the garage where I took my car for service. I know from a consulting perspective that in this dealership franchise levels of employee loyalty, in the sense of how long they have been with the organization, are very high. The majority of employees had worked for the organization for over 15 years. However, as my experience of their service shows, staying loyal to an organization and being entirely satisfied at work does not necessarily mean that employees will strive to 'wow' the customer or give a great service.

In fact if anything, my experience of this particular organization is that it is set in its ways, procedure bound and averse to change. It lacks innovation, energy and drive. As a consequence, it is losing market share to its more aggressive competitors. A high proportion of employees were either cynical in their views towards the organization or exhibited 'victim' behaviour. This manifests itself in inertia and a widespread believe that 'the grass is greener on the other side' – people in other organizations are better off than those in this particular business, but the employees lack the energy to do anything about it.

So my issue with just measuring and focusing on satisfaction and what might be perceived as loyalty is that although the majority of employees may like their work, they may not necessarily be motivated to give discretionary effort. Research by organizations such as Gallup shows that on average no matter how long employees stay with an organization or how satisfied they are with their job, only 29 per cent are typically fully engaged with the company and willing to give discretionary effort. Another 49 per cent will be indifferent and 22 per cent actively disengaged.

Companies with disengaged staff can be spotted by:

▌ high staff turnover;

▌ high absenteeism;

▌ high stress levels;

▌ the difficulty they have reaching decisions;

▌ lack of effective communication;

▌ political in-fighting;

▌ badly communicated company values.

Some employees can be loyal to an organization and satisfied with their job; therefore they may not demonstrate pride, passion and energy to deliver more on behalf of their organization. An example of this is in the public health sector. My observation is that many employees here are self-motivated and dedicated professionals who get satisfaction from their job but do not feel particularly engaged with the organization that employs them. They may relate well to their patients and their needs and take a professional pride in their job, but they disassociate themselves from their employer. Some do not agree with the decisions that are taken by the management of the organization. They may not believe that their voices are heard.

So to clarify, employee engagement is about the 'oomph' factor that employees bring to their jobs. To encourage them to do this means developing and implementing strategies to satisfy, engage and retain employees. Walt Disney World Management, for example, recognize that engaged employees lead to higher levels of engaged customers. Their philosophy towards employees is:

- Make them feel special.

- Treat them as individuals.

- Respect them.

- Make them knowledgeable.

THE BENEFITS OF EMPLOYEE ENGAGEMENT

Employee engagement is not an easy issue to tackle. However, if you get it right there are great prizes to be had.

I imagine you will be reading this book if you want to increase the level of engagement in your organization. The first two questions that you may encounter when you try to convince others of this approach could be: So why should our organization be focusing on this? What are the potential business benefits?'

There have been a number of research studies across a wide range of industries and countries as to the benefits of employee engagement.

As proof that engagement works, in this section I have listed some of the key research findings indicating that companies with higher levels of employee engagement outperform their rivals in terms of profitability.

- According to research by professional services company Towers Perrin, organizations with higher levels of employee engagement outperform their competitors in terms of performance and profitability on aggregate by 17 per cent. Although the study does not prove a direct causality between employee engagement and profitability because it recognizes that the number of variables is too great, it does state that evidence of a significant relationship between employee engagement and financial performance is undeniable.

- Sirota Consulting in the United States studied 28 multinational companies throughout 2004 and found that the share prices of organizations with highly engaged employees rose by an average of 16 per cent, compared to an industry average of 6 per cent.

- Studies show that a 10 per cent increase in employee engagement leads to a 6 per cent increase in customer satisfaction and a 2 per cent increase in profitability.

▌ An ISR study published in August 2005 showed that companies with low levels of employee engagement saw net profit fall by 1.38 per cent and operating margin fall by 2.01 per cent over a 36-month period. In companies with above average levels of employee engagement profits rose by 2.06 per cent and operating margin rose by 3.74 per cent in the same 36-month period.

▌ The Hay Group found that professional services organizations with engaged employees were up to 43 per cent more productive.

▌ Gallup research showed engaged employees are more productive, more customer focused, less likely to leave the organization and more profitable than their counterparts.

▌ In 2002 Watson Wyatt found that high-commitment organizations outperformed those with low commitment by 47 per cent.

▌ Stanford University suggests that employee commitment results in corporate performance gains of between 30 and 40 per cent.

▌ According to the DDI research study 'Predicting Employee Engagement 2005' (see www.ddiworld.com), highly engaged individuals are 33 per cent less likely to leave their organization within the next year.

Creating the conditions where employees feel able to give of their best therefore results in documented benefits such as:

▌ greater productivity;

▌ increased passion for and commitment to the organization's vision, strategy and goals;

▌ greater alignment with the organization's values;

▌ a high-energy working environment;

▌ a greater sense of team;

▌ higher levels of creativity and innovation;

▌ a greater sense of loyalty to the organization;

▌ higher staff retention, lowered attrition rate;

▌ better recruitment and selection;

▌ higher talent retention;

▌ employees being better brand ambassadors;

▌ attractive reputation;

▌ improved customer experience and customer loyalty;

▌ boosted business growth;

▌ greater value creation;

▌ sustained, long-term success.

Ultimately, research continues to show a well-substantiated relationship between employee engagement and business results which goes beyond satisfaction and loyalty.

Conversely, research by Gallup shows a tendency for actively disengaged employees to be significantly less productive than their engaged colleagues, show lower levels of customer focus and less loyalty to their organizations.

So it is now a generally acknowledged business fact that employee engagement is a key driver of business success. When asked which measurements 'give the best sense of a company's health' in a *Business Week* advice column, former GE Chairman and CEO Jack Welch replied:

> Employee engagement first. It goes without saying that no company, small or large, can win over the long run without energized employees who believe in the mission and understand how to achieve it. That's why you need to take a measure of employee engagement at least once a year through anonymous surveys in which people feel completely safe to speak their minds.

This is a view shared by Leary-Joyce, who works with the *Sunday Times* on its annual list of the 100 best companies to work for. She says: 'The only thing your competitors cannot copy – your only truly unique and lasting competitive edge – is your people. Your people really are your greatest asset. Or they will be if you build a work environment in which they can shine.' (Leary-Joyce, 2004)

EMPLOYEE ENGAGEMENT AND HUMAN CAPITAL MANAGEMENT

If you are from the HR profession or working as an agent for change in your organization, it may be useful to know that employee engagement is part of a trend towards human capital management (HCM). This is the strategy that an organization adopts to put people at its heart. The last decade has seen a sea of change in finance directors' views of what constitutes the asset base of their organization. They have moved towards recognizing organizational factors (such as brand image), and customer, employee and supplier factors as assets (not costs and liabilities) and are looking at methods of reporting these alongside the traditional physical and financial asset accounting on their balance sheets.

Human capital is a component part of the 'intellectual capital' of a company, which is linked to the difference between the market value and book value of a company. Recent estimates suggest that 50 to 90 per cent of the value created by an organization comes not from the management of traditional physical assets, but from the management of intellectual capital. As John Sunderland, Executive Chairman, Cadbury Schweppes describes: 'An organization's success is the product of its people competence. That link between people and performance should be made visible and available to all stakeholders.'

Some countries (predominantly in Europe) are passing legislation to make it a requirement to report on organizational assets. In the United States, although this is not a legal requirement in accountancy terms, the law does order every government agency to appoint a chief human capital officer (CHCO). The human capital chiefs are in charge of getting the right people in the right place at the right time. Their duties include writing workforce development strategies, analysing workforce needs, aligning human resources policies with agencies' missions and goals, advocating continuous learning, identifying best practices in human resources, measuring intellectual capital, and advising agency heads on hiring, developing, training and managing.

In the United Kingdom a government-backed think tank, the HCM Standards Group, has been formed to promote issues of HCM. Formed by Investors in People (IiP) UK, the HCM Standards Group aims to explore a set of universal principles for comparing companies' human capital. The ultimate goal is to develop a set of reporting standards for human capital. Recent statistics from IiP suggest that one in four managers thinks HCM reporting should be made mandatory, and that 60 per cent of organizations are already measuring their human capital in some way.

'It is intriguing that so many companies say people are their greatest asset, but even companies with a reputation for achieving a great deal in this area tell their investors next to nothing about what they are doing', said Rob Lake, head of corporate engagement at Henderson Global Investors. 'If companies think they have a story to tell, why aren't they telling it to their investors?'

Ruth Spellman, chief executive of IiP UK, wrote in an article in _People Management_, 27 July 2006:

Employers should view HCM as much more than just a reporting mechanism, as it can help them to identify strengths and weaknesses in the way they equip and support employees to make the contribution expected of them. It's a great way of aligning people with business performance; employers that don't make this connection will fail to get the real business benefits HCM can deliver.

EMPLOYEE ENGAGEMENT AND THE PERCEPTION OF THE HR FUNCTION

Still today the perception of senior managers in some organizations is that HR is not a corporate function that adds value to the business. Sales and operations have far more 'clout' at the board table of some organizations and people issues are sometimes not given much air time. So what is in it for you if you champion employee engagement as an HR professional or change agent?

As the trend to recognize HCM increases, so does the emphasis on employee engagement. This has implications for HR departments. By focusing on engagement you can better engage with the business at a strategic level. By focusing on engagement you move away from the traditional approach of HR management (HRM) where employees are seen as a cost and need to be controlled and rewarded. The HCM approach to employees is that they are assets that need to be nurtured and developed. Figure 1.8 shows examples of the differences between HCM and HRM.

IS EMPLOYEE ENGAGEMENT WORTH THE INVESTMENT?

As the business world and in particular the HR community becomes more aware of the benefits of engagement, analysts predict that employee engagement will become a key measure of organizational success. Already employee engagement is replacing employee satisfaction in the majority of businesses as a key measure of success and it will continue to grow in importance in the future.

For example, in the latest *Sunday Times* list of best companies to work for, winning organizations with high levels of engagement now take pole position in the FTSE 100 in terms of increased profits (12.4 per cent over six years, higher than those who didn't make the list). Below are two case studies: one a small-to-medium sized enterprise (SME) in the United

Human capital management (HCM)	HR management (HRM)
Regards employees as an organizational asset	Regards employees as a costly resource
People practices are aligned to and supportive of organizational strategy	People practices are based on the transactions in the employee life cycle
Views line managers as customers and creates effective partnerships	Creates a 'burden' for line managers (eg by giving them onerous performance management systems to operate)
Focuses on developing employee engagement and commitment to the organization via participation and involvement	Focuses on getting employee cooperation via a system of command/control and reward
Treats the cause of human performance problems	Treats the symptoms of human performance problems
Recognises 'self-motivation factors' (eg values and behaviours, work–life balance)	Focuses on the 'hygiene factors' (eg pay and benefits, health and safety)

Figure 1.8 Differences between HCM and HRM

Kingdom, the other a large IT organization in India, both of which have seen results via focusing on employee engagement.

Case studies

W L Gore

There are no magic formulas as each culture and environment is different. W L Gore, for example, has three times come highest in the *Sunday Times* list of the 100 best companies to work for. Positive scores from staff for belief in the values of the organization, pride in working for Gore, being able to make a difference and loving their jobs at 93 per cent, 93 per cent, 92 per cent and 90 per cent are all top results. Yet it would be difficult to replicate the Gore approach. Gore is a Scottish-based company with products ranging from bagpipes to dental floss, spacesuits to guitar strings. Gore-Tex is its most famous creation. The pioneering fabric is both water-tight and breathable. Gore employs 425 personnel in two sites in Livingston and one in Dundee.

The company was launched by US couple Bill and Vieve Gore in 1958. All employees are associates, not directors, secretaries or managers, and teamwork is so important that colleagues' rating of each other is one of the things pay is based on. The high satisfaction rates reflect the positive response to the non-hierarchical environment created by Bill Gore, who believed this would encourage creativity. This is a title-free organization. 'It makes us a very productive place to work', says John Kennedy, the company's UK representative. 'We believe in the individual. If you treat them right they will do good things.' (*Sunday Times*, March 2006)

John Kennedy, who has no job title but is responsible for all UK associates, thinks what differentiates Gore from everyone else is its culture. He explains:

> It's belief in the individual. We try to let people do things they are good at as opposed to forcing them into things they are not good at. A lot of why we have been successful is down to the way we treat people and how people react to that. It works for us and makes us a good place to work and a very productive place to work.

Would-be associates can expect to spend up to eight hours being interviewed over as many as three days. Careful selection appears to pay off; more than half the staff have worked at the company for at least 10 years and Gore gets another top score of 75 per cent for staff saying they have their dream job.

Innovation is the only constant at W L Gore and that suits staff; they would strongly recommend the company as a place to work (with a 95 per cent positive score) and think their job is good for personal growth (92 per cent); they feel they are trusted to do their job by their leaders (90 per cent), who are excellent role models (80 per cent).

The firm, which made a profit of £14.6 million last financial year on its UK revenue of £105.9 million, spent £48,000 on social events and supports workers in charity events. Benefits include a final salary pension scheme, 26 weeks' fully paid maternity leave and private healthcare. There is a share option scheme and profit-related pay. Flexible working allows staff to balance responsibilities at home and work. Few feel they are taken advantage of; the 80 per cent positive score here is the highest, as is the 91 per cent score for health not suffering because of work.

Infosystems

India is one of the fastest growing economies in the world, with burgeoning technological prowess and a myriad of businesses. Experts predict that by 2010 it will be the third most powerful economy in the world after the United States and China. In India many businesses are now becoming aware of the need to engage their employees. Best practice organizations have a range of initiatives to improve engagement levels. Indian IT consultancy Infosystems has undertaken a range of projects starting at the selection stage. These include:

- choosing the right fit and giving a realistic job preview;

- a strong induction and orientation programme;

- rigorous training and development, from technical to soft skills to leadership development programmes;

- incentives such as recognition letters, profit-sharing schemes, long performance awards;

- giving regular feedback to all people;

- communication forums like the in-house magazine _Intouch_, an e-forum to develop entrepreneurship and regular surveys and conferences;

- recreational activities like festivities, get-togethers and sport, to maintain the quality of work life and a balance between personal and professional life.

The intention is to build an open and transparent culture to empower its people and develop entrepreneurs. 'The result of these practices is evident through the regular feedback from our employees collected through conferences and surveys, apart from the employee engagement survey conducted every second year. The proof is the latest increase in employee engagement in two years from 54 per cent to 64 per cent', says Vivek Punekar, Associate Vice-president, HRD, HCL Infosystems in a Vertex web article.

Raising engagement levels, and maintaining them, takes time, effort, commitment and investment. Engagement is a two-way process: organizations must work to engage the employee, who in turn has a choice about the level of engagement to offer the employer.

Embarking on a drive to increase engagement levels should not be undertaken lightly, bearing in mind the ease with which engagement (like the psychological contract) can be shattered. The challenge for companies seeking to improve engagement levels is to determine the unique elements of the work experience that are most likely to influence engagement in the country or region in which they operate.

This book can help you do this as you read through each chapter. Before you do this, however, it may be useful to clarify what you wish to gain both as an organization and personally from undertaking an employee engagement initiative.

Checklist

What are benefits of employee engagement for your business?

What do you hope to gain?

In your role of HR professional, consultant, manager or change agent you will need to convince your business partners of the benefits of employee engagement to the organization. Use this checklist to clarify and record your thoughts on what you hope to gain from increasing levels of engagement.

Thinking about your business partners, what will they perceive as the key organizational benefits of employee engagement?

What business issues will employee engagement address for your organization?

What do you hope to gain from a personal and professional perspective in championing employee engagement?

This chapter has explained what employee engagement is, as well as outlining the benefits of employee engagement to the organization. It has described the rise of the 'engagement' phenomenon and whether this is a trend that is set to grow. It has also discussed the link between employee engagement and customer engagement. In the next chapter I outline how to go about setting up an employee engagement programme.

2

Beginning an employee engagement programme

Now that we have looked at what engagement means and the benefits it can bring, this second chapter addresses routes to beginning an employee engagement programme and the type of data you can collect to measure where you currently are.

GAINING BUY-IN

Imagine my surprise when shortly after my visit to the opticians, I was contacted by the organization's HR director in my role as a consultant. The HR director and I began discussions about the need to help them become more customer focused.

The HR director explained that the organization had recently acquired a smaller high street chain and the CEO had plans to expand further and develop the brand. Like all retailers the organization had a high proportion of part-time workers. Attrition rates were high but no more or less than other retailers'. However, the CEO was concerned on two fronts: the number of customer complaints they were receiving was rising and the organization was finding it increasingly difficult to attract and retain good people. Likewise, the HR director was keen to establish the organization as an employer of choice. Both the HR director and the CEO had anecdotal evidence that since the takeover some of staff had actively disengaged from the organization.

Having held discussions with both the HR director and the CEO, I found that they were both keen to develop an employee engagement strategy, although neither called it by that name. The key, however, was that they both recognized that ultimately the more committed an employee was to the organization and actively engaged with the brand, the more engaged the customer was likely to be.

The HR director had done some ground work in researching the topic and had gathered some data about the effect on increased levels of employee engagement. There are several case studies that illustrate the financial benefits of engagement. For example, the construction equipment maker Caterpillar documented significant savings as a result of increases in the levels of employee engagement. The company registered:

- an annual saving of US $8.8 million from decreased attrition, absenteeism and overtime at a European plant over a year;

- a US $2 million increase in profit and 34 per cent increase in customer satisfaction at a start-up plant over a year;

- a 70 per cent increase in output in less than four months in an Asian plant.

At the beverage company Molson Coors, plants where employee engagement scores were high were seven times less likely to have a safety incident which lost the company time They also found that sales teams whose employee engagement scores were low fell behind their highly engaged counterparts by on average US $2.1 million over one year. The HR director of the option chain shared this background information with other members of the senior management team, most of whom are favourable to the idea of starting a programme of employee engagement. Based on this canvassed opinion, it was agreed that at the next meeting of the executive the HR director would outline to the members of the senior management team some of the potential benefits of employee engagement and present a business case.

At the meeting there was a healthy debate, and some doubt was expressed by a few members of the senior management team about whether employee engagement should be a priority issue for the board. However, the CEO was on board and it was agreed that the next step should be for the HR director to develop a strategy to address levels of employee engagement.

Key learning points

▌ When developing an employee engagement strategy ensure that you canvass opinions from the senior management team to see where your supporters lie.

▌ Seek a high-level sponsor who is prepared to give you support in terms of time and energy to spearhead the programme.

▌ Discuss the benefits of the programme from a business perspective and develop a sound business case.

▌ Use hard evidence of the impact of employee engagement on other businesses to support your case.

▌ Relate the potential business benefits to your organizational context.

THE STARTING POINT

Imagine that your CEO has asked you to develop an employee engagement strategy. Where do you begin?

The starting point for improving employee engagement is to assess where the organization is currently. You will need this information to draw later comparisons in order to assess the impact of your employee engagement programme. You probably have data already available to you to start this process. There are various ways in which you can evaluate the current levels of engagement. These include:

▌ engagement surveys – tailored to your organization or using proprietary benchmark studies;

▌ 'pulse' or ad hoc surveys;

▌ recruitment surveys to track turnover and levels of engagement of new recruits during the first 30, 90 and 180 days of employment;

▌ attrition rates;

▌ absenteeism rates;

▌ performance/quality ratings;

▌ diversity/equality rates;

▌ number of training days per employee;

- percentage of employees with a personal development plan;
- numbers of people receiving coaching and mentoring;
- ratio of internal to external hires;
- benchmark studies.

My advice is to review any information that you have of this kind to gain a picture of where the organization is now.

3M case study

3M has a worldwide reputation for high-quality products. Renowned for its innovations, the global company uses a number of methods to measure its employee engagement. Every business unit worldwide surveys their entire organization once every two years using the 'Standard opinion survey'. The survey allows employees to candidly express their views about 3M, their business unit and their jobs, in complete confidentiality. In addition a 'Leadership survey' is administered to leaders worldwide. The purpose of the surveys is to establish benchmarks for the future, evaluate current key corporate initiatives and to help target areas for action. In addition employee focus groups are regularly held. And employee input weighs heavily in management actions.

MEASURING EMPLOYEE ENGAGEMENT

In the case of the optician retailer, although some of this material was available, we agreed that to help us develop a strategy and as a means of benchmarking for the future we would conduct an employee engagement survey.

Establishing current levels of employee engagement is many organizations' first step in defining an engagement plan. Surveying helps you establish where you are now versus where you want to be. The results of this type of audit can help you develop a strategy and plan of action to increase levels of engagement.

At present it is estimated that about 50 per cent of Fortune 500 companies in the United States conduct formal employee engagement surveys on a periodic basis, typically every two years. In addition, thousands of smaller companies also conduct such surveys. I recommend that an engagement survey should be conducted at least every year and that a robust action plan be developed to address the issues raised.

EMPLOYEE ENGAGEMENT SURVEYS

Best practice shows that it is useful to undertake an employee engagement survey on a regular basis, even if the economic climate is challenging.

Bacardi-Martini case study

The Southampton-based drinks manufacturing company Bacardi-Martini has a strong record of engagement as measured in the *Sunday Times* survey of the 100 best companies to work for. It was ranked in the top 10 for the first five annual contests, dropping just outside to 15th place in 2006. But John Beard, the chief executive, is more proud of the 2006 year's achievement than any other. This is because it was accomplished while the business underwent its first redundancies in almost 30 years, as well as the departure of its former chief executive.

The losses were due to the alcopops industry cooling and the consequent drop in Bacardi Breezer sales. In all, 30 people were made redundant, although just one redundancy was compulsory. In an article in the *Sunday Times* (March, 2006), Beard said:

> For sound commercial reasons, we had to go through a redundancy programme. That was quite a shock for the business culture. We had a big debate on how the redundancies would impact on our Best Companies performance, and my view was that this is when it counts.

Key learning points

▍ If you are going to measure employee engagement, ensure that you do this on a regular basis, for example annually.

▍ Continue to measure in bad times as well as in good – the results will help you develop a robust employee engagement strategy.

The optician retailer had to decide how it would survey its employees. Never having done this before it decided to turn to an external provider and to use a standard survey.

PROPRIETARY SURVEYS

One of the considerations when intending to undertake some form of measurement of current levels of employee engagement is whether to develop your own survey or to use an external provider. There are a number of well-respected organizations that have developed a series of metrics to measure employee engagement both on a national and international basis. Most engagement studies invite employees to answer a number of short survey questions indicating their level of agreement with different statements about the organization and their work. This feedback is conducted on an anonymous basis. Scores are aggregated to provide a view of the level of engagement at an organizational level as well as engagement scores for each function or department. The same questions should be repeated on a biannual or annual basis so that progress can be tracked.

Some of the businesses that provide this type of service include Institute of Employment Studies, The Hay Group, Gallup, IES and Towers Perrins.

For example, the Institute of Employment Studies (IES) used data from over 10,000 employees in 14 organizations in the United Kingdom working in the National Health Service (NHS). They developed 12 attitude statements representing engagement and combined these to arrive at a single indicator of employee engagement. The research methodology was subsequently proved reliable and valid for organizations other than the NHS and is now widely applied. Towers Perrins conduct an annual study of employee engagement. This reaches roughly 86,000 people working full time for large and medium-sized companies in 16 countries across four continents. Gallup has developed a proprietary formula to measure levels of employee engagement based on worldwide survey results and performance data in its database. Its employee engagement consulting practice has surveyed more than 1.5 million employees at more than 87,000 divisions or work units. The results allow their clients to see and understand links between levels of employee engagement and productivity, growth and profitability.

At the end of this book I list the contact details for these organizations. All are very experienced in developing employee engagement surveys in both the public and the private sector. The benefit of using these or similar providers is that they can benchmark your organization nationally and globally. The downside is that these surveys can be expensive to run. It is worth also investigating local suppliers who may not have such extensive databases of benchmarked organizations but who still may have the expertise to help you develop a robust survey.

When choosing a potential supplier consider what experience they have in this area and how they can add value to your organization. It is worth speaking to other organizations who have used their services as well as making sure that the survey methodologies that they propose to use are suitable for your organizational environment. A further consideration is whether the provider will consult you after the survey has been completed to give you expert advice on key priorities for improvement.

DIFFERENT LEVELS OF EMPLOYEE ENGAGEMENT

If you do decide to use a proprietary survey to benchmark your organization, be aware of the variables that exist when making comparisons with other organizations. Research shows that demographics can impact the degree to which people are engaged, which ranges from active engagement through indifference to active disengagement.

Most studies therefore indicate the variances that there are between the levels of engagement that are found among the employee population. The Towers Perrins study, for example, talks about engaged employees as those who put in consistent extra effort to improve customer service, manage costs and meet other critical business objectives essential to improved performance. It estimates that only 14 per cent of employees worldwide are fully engaged on the job. Towers Perrins estimate that the vast majority of employees are moderately engaged at best. Perhaps most disturbingly, they estimate that nearly a quarter are actively disengaged. Gallup cites similar figures based on its research studies.

Within these figures there can be many variables. The IES study of employee engagement in the NHS, for example, found that engagement levels fell if employees had had an accident or an injury at work or if they had experienced harassment. The IES research in this sector also indicated that engagement levels fell as employees got older. The study in the NHS found that the management population were more likely to be engaged than more junior members of staff. Employees of minority ethnic backgrounds were also more highly engaged than other colleagues. IES also found relatively high levels of engagement among the over 60s, suggesting sources of untapped potential in some organizations.

On a country-by-country basis, levels of engagement vary considerably. The Towers Perrins 'Global Workforce Study', for example, records the highest levels of engagement in Mexico (40 per cent) and Brazil (31 per cent), whereas only 8 per cent of Chinese employees in their survey were highly engaged.

Another interesting finding from the Chartered Institute of Personnel and Development in the United Kingdom is that younger people (the so-called generation X) are less engaged than over 35s. Under 35s want a sense of excitement, a sense of community and a life outside work. They are not interested in a job for life and do not expect the organization to offer this to them.

So a robust employee engagement survey should be able to indicate variances between levels of engagement and different employee groups in an organization. I recommend therefore that any survey you undertake is broken down by relevant function and/or line manager, since within each organization there will be varying micro-climates.

Interesting also are the country, regional and cultural differences that impact on levels of engagement. For example, a study showed that in the United States a high driver of engagement was competitive health benefits; in Canada the top driver of employee engagement was seen in a recent study to be base pay, work–life balance and career advancement opportunities; in India focus on reputation of the organization as a good employer; in Germany the level of autonomy; in the Netherlands the collaborative environment; and in Japan the calibre of co-workers.

Key learning points

▌ It is helpful to benchmark your organization's levels of engagement with other businesses in a similar market or sector.

▌ Be aware that different groups are likely to have different levels of engagement and therefore differing needs. There are micro-climates in each organization.

▌ You will need to decide whether to run the survey across the whole organization or to ask a sample of employees from different parts of the organization to complete the survey. My personal view is that it is best for everyone to complete the survey. It sends a positive signal to employees that you are interested in their opinions and it allows you to benchmark different parts of the organization and to identify best practice.

ASSESS YOUR CURRENT LEVELS OF EMPLOYEE ENGAGEMENT

A more cost-effective way of running an employee engagement survey can be to develop one yourself if you have the internal resources to do so. If you do decide not to use an external employee engagement survey but to develop one of your own, I recommend that you establish a working party made up from employees from different parts of the business to help do this.

They can agree the types of questions to be asked as part of the survey and how the survey will be communicated and disseminated. Do not underestimate how important it is to position the survey well, to explain fully the reasons why you are running it and to assure confidentiality. It is also helpful to have a dedicated resource internally who can collate the results.

If you do decide to go down the survey route, when you ask people to complete the self-assessment, stress that there are no right or wrong answers. It is essential that the survey is completed anonymously so that people feel that they can answer honestly. It is acceptable, however, to ask for business function or area so you gain a true picture of the variations of levels of engagement are in your organization.

Below are examples of the type of questions that I recommend that you cover. You can add to or tailor the questions to suit your particular environment.

EXAMPLE ENGAGEMENT SURVEY QUESTIONS

Please indicate your agreement on a scale of 1 to 10 to the following questions: 1 and 2 indicate 'very strongly disagree' and 9 and 10 indicate 'very strongly agree'. There are no right or wrong answers, your honest opinions count.

Section 1

1. The organization recruits and selects the right people to the right jobs.

   Your score out of 10: _____

2. I receive appropriate training and development to help me do my job well.

   Your score out of 10: _____

3. I have a personal development plan that helps me grow and develop my career.

   Your score out of 10: _____

4. I have ample opportunity to develop my skills, knowledge and behaviours.

   Your score out of 10: _____

5. I am given the appropriate level of authority to do a good job.

   Your score out of 10: _____

6. I am satisfied with the opportunities there are to develop my career.

   Your score out of 10: _____

7. The organization recognizes and develops people's talents.

   Your score out of 10: _____

8. I receive appropriate pay and benefits for the job I do.

   Your score out of 10: _____

9. In the past month I have received praise and recognition for a job well done.

   Your score out of 10: _____

10. My manager reviews my performance with me on a one-to-one basis at least once every six months.

    Your score out of 10: _____

Section 2

11. My immediate line manager makes me feel my contributions are valued.

    Your score out of 10: _____

12. I feel appropriately involved in decision making.

    Your score out of 10: _____

13. I am able to voice my views to my manager.

    Your score out of 10: _____

14. My manager listens to and acts on my views.

    Your score out of 10: _____

15. Managers in this organization encourage two-way communication that promotes open and honest dialogue and understanding.

    Your score out of 10: _____

16. Teamwork is encouraged in my work unit/department.

    Your score out of 10: _____

17. The organization promotes internal cooperation.

    Your score out of 10: _____

18. I feel part of a family working for this organization.

    Your score out of 10: _____

19. I trust my colleagues to do a good job.

    Your score out of 10: _____

20. I am encouraged to come up with new ways of doing things.

    Your score out of 10: _____

Section 3

21. My immediate line manager cares for me as a person.

    Your score out of 10: _____

22. This organization makes an effective contribution to the community.

    Your score out of 10: _____

23. This organization promotes equal opportunities.

    Your score out of 10: _____

24. I am not overloaded with work to do.

    Your score out of 10: _____

25. I have appropriately stimulating and challenging work.

    Your score out of 10: _____

26. The organization promotes the health and well-being of employees.

    Your score out of 10: _____

27. I am happy with my work–life balance.

    Your score out of 10: _____

28. The organization has appropriate family-friendly policies.

    Your score out of 10: _____

29. I have the appropriate resources to do my job well.

    Your score out of 10: _____

30. I can relate to the values of this organization.

    Your score out of 10: _____

Section 4

31. Communication across the organization is effective.

    Your score out of 10: _____

32. The goals of this organization are clear.

    Your score out of 10: _____

33. I receive timely information to help me do my job well.

    Your score out of 10: _____

34. I have trust in the leaders of this organization.

    Your score out of 10: _____

35. I have a clear understanding of the vision of this organization.

    Your score out of 10: _____

36. The job that I do adds value to the organization.

    Your score out of 10: _____

37. I am clear what is expected of me in my role.

    Your score out of 10: _____

38. Senior managers lead by example.

    Your score out of 10: _____

39. I am informed at appropriate intervals about what our customers think about us.

    Your score out of 10: _____

40. I am aware of the values of the organization.

    Your score out of 10: _____

Section 5

41. I am proud to work for this organization.

    Your score out of 10: _____

42. I would recommend this organization to others as a good place to work.

    Your score out of 10:_____

43. I care about the future of this organization.

    Your score out of 10:_____

44. I would recommend to my friends and family that they do business with this organization.

    Your score out of 10:_____

45. I am willing to go the extra mile on behalf of the organization.

    Your score out of 10:_____

POSITIONING THE SURVEY

The HR director of the optician retailer decided to set up a working party with representatives from across the business to manage the survey. Importantly, they trialled the questionnaire with a sample of a dozen people to make sure that the questions and format were clear. The working party suggested that the easiest way to disseminate the survey was via employees' salary envelopes. This was because people working in the retail environment had limited access to a computer and therefore could not complete the survey online.

This was the first time that the business had undertaken a survey which involved all employees, although parts of the organization had experience of this in the past. Unfortunately, the response rate to the survey was only 30 per cent. This was far less than the expected. The average response rate to employee surveys is normally 65 per cent and in some organizations it is much higher, for example the RBS Group measure 150,000 people in 30 countries over 40 brands and have a response rate of 87 per cent overall and 94 per cent online.

In the optician retailer's case, the response rate itself seemed to be a clear indication of employee engagement. To discover the reason for the poor response rate, the chain held a series of focus groups with employees to find out more about what employees really felt about the organization.

Financial services organization First Direct, for example, believes it must continue to work at understanding its employees and the culture more deeply using a variety of methods. It has introduced a 'culture critique', using staff focus groups, written surveys and one-to-one interviews with not just current employees but past ones too.

If you are going to run focus groups to canvass opinions before or after the survey, make sure that they are run by expert facilitators. People will not be forthcoming if they know the facilitator well or if they think that the person is not independent or may misrepresent their views.

In the case of the optician retailer, focus groups that were subsequently run by independent facilitators discovered from employees that the low response rates were due to lack of briefing by line managers. There was also a lot of suspicion that the results of the survey would not truly be anonymous. In addition, people were not willing to fill in the questionnaire at home with their pay packet in their own time and they had not been allocated any time at work to do this. The focus groups did, however, have a positive impact. Members of staff began voicing some of their concerns about the organization and its practices, particularly in light of the recent takeover. They expressed concern about the lack of clear vision or direction of the organization and the heavy-handed ways in which the takeover had been implemented. The outputs of the focus groups were collated and categorized so that senior managers could see what was really important to employees.

Key learning points

▌ Ensure that employees are well briefed about the survey.

▌ Offer different options for how employees can complete the survey, for example online or via a dedicated time slot at work if completing a paper version.

▌ Use a variety of different methods to surface employees' opinions and don't just rely on a questionnaire.

▌ Involve a cross-section of employees in the design and development of the employee engagement survey.

▌ If using a questionnaire remember to pilot it before full distribution.

▌ Develop a communications strategy for informing employers about the survey.

▌ Ensure that people know *why* the survey is being undertaken and *what* will be done with the results.

▌ Involve line managers in briefing staff about the survey.

▌ Allocate time at work for employees to complete the survey.

Checklist

What measurements of engagement are right for your business?

What measures do you currently have of employee engagement in your business? Indicate if you have these and then rate the appropriateness of each measure. Examples include:

- engagement surveys;
- 'pulse' or ad hoc surveys;
- recruitment surveys;
- attrition rates;
- absenteeism rates;
- performance/quality ratings;
- diversity/equality rates;
- number of training days per employee;
- percentage of employees with a personal development plan;
- numbers of people receiving coaching and mentoring;
- ratio of internal to external hires;
- benchmark data.

What additional quantitative and qualitative methods should you use to measure levels of engagement in your business?

This chapter has outlined the starting point for an employee engagement programme. This should be to review the current levels of engagement in the business. If you have not got sufficient data, then undertaking an employee engagement survey is a first step. This can be either developed in-house or by using proprietary surveys. The survey will be successful if it is communicated well and gives you both quantitative and qualitative data. In the next chapter I outline how to manage the outputs of an employee opinion survey and develop an employee engagement strategy.

3

Identifying the key drivers of engagement for your business

This chapter provides you with pointers on how to identify the key drivers of employee engagement in your business.

USING THE RESULTS OF EMPLOYEE ENGAGEMENT SURVEYS

So if, like the chain of optician retailers, you have undertaken an employee engagement survey and benchmarked your organization's levels of engagement, how do you use the results to develop an employee engagement strategy? The key is to identify the drivers, or 'hot buttons' of employee engagement in your business.

As researchers point out, not all workers want the same thing:

Some care deeply about the social connections formed in the workplace, others want to make as much money with as much flexibility and as little commitment as possible. Some have an appetite for risk. Others crave the steadiness of a well-structured, long term climb up the career ladder. (Erickson and Grafton, *Harvard Business Review*, 2007).

If you simply look at the results of an engagement survey as a whole, without analysing the needs of different workers, you are in danger of applying a blanket approach to what is a complex topic. Furthermore, unless you discover what is *important* to each target group, you may increase the volume on certain aspects of work but the music may be falling on deaf ears.

Using follow-up focus groups is a good method in helping identification of the key drivers of engagement. Once you have received the survey results, for example, you can ask different groups of employees to rank the importance of different factors in increasing their levels of engagement.

First, you need of course to be aware of the different demographics of the diverse groups that make up your organization. For example, research shows that the so-called generation X (the under 35s) have a more detached view of work. For many of them work–life balance and making a difference in the community may be more important than career advancement or financial reward.

To illustrate why establishing the drivers of engagement is important, here are several examples of different organizations.

Case studies

Chrysler Group and BellSouth

Car manufacturer Chrysler Group has identified that the key factors influencing engagement in its business are:

- a collaborative work environment where people work well in teams;
- challenging work;
- input on decision making;
- resources to get the job done;
- authority to make decisions;
- career advancement opportunities;
- the company's reputation as a good employer;
- evidence that the company is focused on customers;
- a clear vision from senior management about future success;
- senior managers' interest in employees' well-being.

Chrysler Group sees the four parts of the jigsaw that leads to engagement as company leaders, supervisors, HR practices and policies, and company communications. Contrast these drivers of engagement with those of Atlanta-based telecommunications company BellSouth. At BellSouth the drivers of employee engagement are seen as:

I affiliation with a company that is seen to be a winner;

I work content – doing work that is challenging and makes a difference;

I having a clear career path;

I benefits – the type of benefits offered such as health plans, stock options, pension plans.

We can see that in these two US organizations, only some of the drivers are the same. It is worthwhile testing what is important to your employees.

Tesco HSC (Hindustan Service Centre)

Sudheesh Venkatesh, Head of Human Resources at Tesco HSC (Hindustan Service Centre), views employee engagement as a psychological association. When the parent company did research on employee engagement in the United Kingdom it found that certain factors made a difference. 'Our early experience in India has been similar', says Venkatesh. Employees want to work for an organization that:

I is successful;

I is legal;

I provides opportunities to grow;

I has managers who help employees.

Key learning points

▌ Establish what aspects of your organization's interaction with its workforce will truly drive employee engagement.

▌ Recognize that different groups of employees have different drivers.

▌ Follow up a quantitative survey with focus groups to help provide qualitative data about employees' views.

FOCUS GROUP DISCUSSION ABOUT ENGAGEMENT

When running focus groups to establish what are the key drivers of employee engagement, ensure that you use trained facilitators who are neutral in their approach. Employees will not give their honest opinions if they believe the facilitator is biased. It is a skill to ensure that everyone in a focus group has their say and participants are not influenced by more vocal members of the group.

To establish the key drivers, take the areas that scored poorly in the survey and hold a discussion about the reason why. Invite participants to undertake an exercise to identify which aspects they would most like to see changed that would make a difference to their engagement scores. One way to do this is to ask the group to rate the importance of each particular aspect and then the impact on them personally if the change they would like to see did not happen. You might wish to do this exercise at the end of the focus group. Just before they leave, ask participants to write on a piece of paper what they personally believe needs to change in order to make them feel more engaged with the organization. In this way participants can give their true opinions without being influenced by others. Collect in the results and analyse these as well as what was said in the meeting. Also be aware of 'door handle conversations'. Invariably what is truly on employees' minds comes out just as the group has finished and they are walking to the door!

FEEDING BACK THE RESULTS

Do not expect that the results of an employee engagement survey will be all rosy. At the optician retailer many of the views expressed by staff were unpalatable to senior management. 'It was like holding up a mirror and realizing you were the Wicked Witch, not Snow White after all', said one member of the senior management team.

However, the CEO did recognize that it was important to communicate the results of the survey to employees. Furthermore, the findings put greater emphasis on the need to develop and communicate a strategy and plan of action to bring about improvements. Typically, research indicates that 65 per cent of businesses that undertake surveys ignore the results and take no action.

The optician retailer recognized that it needed not just to feed back the results of the survey but also to involve employees in the development of a strategy for improvement. It established a working party of employees drawn from different parts of the business to help the HR director devise a plan for the way forward. Involving employees at this early stage of strategy development was seen to be very important as many of the lowest scores on the survey related to employee involvement.

Case studies

Looking at examples of how other organizations have dealt with the results of employee surveys there are lessons to be learned. Various case studies from companies that have been successful in this area are set out below.

Arbitron

Call centres throughout the world struggle with engagement and retention of skilled employees. Often the root causes are the lack of challenge in the job, flexibility and career development opportunities. In 2003, the call centre at Arbitron, an international media and marketing research firm, was facing similar employee engagement and talent retention issues.

Arbitron conducts an annual employee engagement survey. In 2003 it was particularly concerned with the survey results from part-time employees, who make up nearly a third of its call centre population. Two areas of particular concern were highlighted as key areas for improvement: career development and employee involvement.

Having received the survey results, the call centre management team led a series of focus groups within the management group and with the call centre employees themselves. Based on the feedback of management and staff, Arbitron's call centre management team set up a cross-functional project team to implement a shortlist of very specific improvement actions. Some actions were simple, inexpensive and quick to fix, others had longer-term implications for the call centre and its culture. Here are a few examples of the feedback received from employees regarding career development and involvement, and the actions taken as a result.

Feedback: Hard to access information on career opportunities in the organization.
Action taken: Moved the job posting board to a more convenient and accessible location.

Feedback: Call centre employees felt they could not advance because they lacked basic computer skills.
Action taken: Offer training in Microsoft Office applications, delivered by full-time staff with strong knowledge of these applications.

Feedback: Employees felt under-informed and less involved.
Action taken: Held regular town hall meetings to discuss current employee issues and monitor the progress of action plan implementation.

The following year's results showed a marked increase in the engagement scores.

Employee involvement jumped 12 percentage points in favourability for call centre employees and remained flat for the rest of the organization. Career development increased five percentage points in favourability for call centre employees but decreased by three points for other employees. A 10 percentage point increase occurred in favourability for the training theme for call centre employees, but there was no change in the training theme for the rest of the organization.

Arbitron attributed the increase in its engagement scores to the commitment of the management team in leading change, the involvement of employees in the improvement project team and creating short-term wins.

Cargill

Cargill Inc, an international provider of food, agricultural and risk management products and services, has been running employee engagement surveys for the past five years and takes the topic very seriously. A new leadership team was introduced into a division after a spate of acquisitions. The engagement survey identified a large drop in the trust that employees felt for the senior management team. In order to increase this, the new team committed to personally visiting each of its six international locations to share the results of the survey with employees. The team held a series of small focus groups where people were able to freely discuss with them what they wanted from them. This commitment of time and effort resulted in a doubling of trust levels by the time the next survey was undertaken.

Caterpillar

At US Caterpillar dealership Fabick CAT, each work area created an 'impact plan' as a result of their annual employee engagement survey. The CEO saw that the communication of these plans was key to their effective implementation. The fact that every workgroup had an action plan meant that all employees were focused on improvement. There were generic improvements that the survey identified as well as workgroup specific items. These were elements such as more learning and development opportunities and better and more appropriate recruitment and selection.

International Paper

Engagement is particularly difficult in times of change. International Paper, one of the world's largest manufacturers of paper products, have faced a series of steep competitive threats. Foreign production plus increases in raw material costs and a general decline in Western demand meant that margins were badly hit. Faced with this situation, the company went through a series of downsizing exercises. Senior managers were aware of the need to actively engage the employees who remained with the organization. For the past six years it has run an annual employee engagement survey followed by a series of action plans. The result has been a slow but steady increase in engagement scores in spite of a further round of job cuts. The business took one of the elements that had scored poorly on the survey and every six months focused on improving this. One of the improvement areas was training and development, where a programme of training and mentoring was introduced to up-skill people on the production floor. A further focus was communication. 'Communication advocates' were established to facilitate the smooth flow of information both formally and informally. They suggested increasing the range of communication vehicles that the management team used. Their efforts led to the introduction of telephone and video information dissemination as well as the traditional paper version and monthly meetings.

Lloyds Broking Group

A very successful Lloyd's UK broking group initiated an employee engagement survey to pinpoint a certain unease among staff, despite major growth in its business. Poor communication was identified as a particular demotivator between managers and staff and between operating divisions. This led to missed opportunities for cross-selling and seeming inconsistency. Staff felt their managers needed to show more understanding, recognize and reward hard work, promote team spirit, improve the working environment and provide clear, fairer working conditions.

Over the next four years goals were set in response to the survey to improve business information in particular. A follow-up questionnaire revealed that there had been a major improvement in communications – up nearly 100 per cent from the previous survey – and clients were seeing more unity and consistency across the business.

Royal Bank of Scotland (RBS)

Every year RBS undertakes a global employee engagement survey among 150,000 workers. It asks questions about employees' desire to give discretionary effort to contribute to business success, to say positive things about RBS and to stay with the company. It also looks at local survey results and entry and exit interviews. From these it calculates an engagement index that is shared with managers in each division and business unit. Each unit then is tasked with developing an action plan for improvement. RBS has established a 'human capita board' and a strategy to increase employee engagement. It recognizes that different approaches are needed at different locations and according to length of service and seniority. To help address these needs the HR community has access to a suite of interactive HR tools called the RBS Human Capita Toolkit. Available on the group intranet, this toolkit includes reward and recognition and employee welfare options.

WH Smith Travel

WH Smith is one of the UK's most well-known retailers. Its travel division sells a range of newspapers, magazines, books and convenience items for people at railway stations and airports. The company commissioned OPP consultants to undertake a survey to see which aspects of its engagement with employees could be improved. Clear career progression and open lines of communication were seen to be the biggest areas of development. However, the survey also highlighted some strengths about the company that employees identified. In particular they felt that they had a good relationship with their line managers and could speak to them freely and openly. When the company fed back the results of the survey to employees it made a point of recognizing the strengths that the audit had revealed.

Key learning points

▍ Communicate the findings of any survey to all employees.

▍ Encourage senior leaders to share the results and to discuss freely what improvements employees need.

▍ Set specific organizational goals as a result of the survey.

▍ Involve people in each unit and function in developing improvement actions.

▍ Identify 'quick wins'.

▍ Focus on getting one thing right at a time.

▍ Recognize the positive aspects of the survey as well as the improvement areas.

▍ Communicate progress of action plans on a regular basis.

SUMMARIZING THE FINDINGS

It is useful to summarize the findings of the employee engagement survey in a format that will help to develop a strategy. A SWOT analysis is a helpful and familiar format to do this. This summarizes the findings of the survey in terms of strengths, weaknesses, opportunities and threats. It is possible to prepare this for different segments of the employee population. For example, Figure 3.1 shows an example of a SWOT analysis for one organization's employee engagement survey based on the opinions of employees who have been with the organization for less than three years.

STRENGTHS	WEAKNESSES
Robust recruitment and selection process Good teamwork Initial remuneration package competitive Team meetings keep employees informed Managers approachable	Poor induction process Inconsistent implementation of performance reviews Little training and development Senior managers remote The need to stay in the same position for 18 months seen as hampering career progression
OPPORTUNITIES	THREATS
Improved induction and learning and development opportunities Consistent implementation of one-to-one reviews Review of career progression criteria Creation of personal development plans Review of communication processes used by senior management	High percentage of employees who leave within three years Competitors with more attractive benefits packages

Figure 3.1   Example of a SWOT analysis

IMPORTANCE AND IMPACT

A further method to help identify the priorities for action is to ask participants at the focus group to rate the importance of each of the aspects of the
survey on a scale of 1 to 10. Then ask them to rate the impact on a scale of 1
to 10 of having each aspect. Calculate the average scores for importance
and impact.

Draw a chart with the x axis as impact and the y axis as importance.
Draw in the scale of 1 to 10 on each axis. Now plot the aspects that have
been rated in terms of their impact and importance.

The resulting four-box chart, also referred to as a priority matrix (see
Figure 3.2) will help you prioritize the different aspects of your survey into
areas of:

▌ low importance and low impact = marginals: low priority for action;

▌ high importance and low impact = givens: low priority for action;

▌ low importance and high impact = hidden opportunities: medium
   priority;

▌ high importance and high impact = engagement drivers: high priority
   for action.

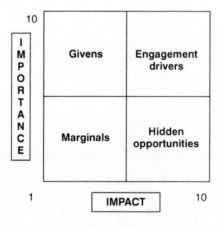

Figure 3.2 Importance versus impact

Checklist

What are the key drivers of employee engagement in your business?

List the key drivers that will improve the levels of employee engagement in your business. Be specific to target populations where appropriate.

How can you identify the key drivers if you have not already done so?

This chapter has outlined the importance of analysing the results of employee engagement surveys and supplementing quantitative results with focus groups. Focus groups allow the organization to identify the key drivers of employee engagement. Different groups are likely to have different drivers of engagement and it is best to address these needs separately. It is important whatever happens to feed back the results of the survey and to prioritize the resulting actions. The next chapter provides a model to help identify which aspects of employee engagement need to form part of your strategy.

4

Developing an employee engagement strategy

This chapter describes how to develop a strategy for employee engagement. It introduces a model of employee engagement called WIFI (well-being, information, fairness, involvement). This should allow you to identify where your organizational strengths are in terms of engagement and areas, based on employee feedback, where you may need to improve. It also looks at how best to set up a programme or project to implement improvements in levels of employee engagement.

You will probably find, as did my optician retailer friends, that when you come to develop a strategy for engagement, there are a number of strands that need to be addressed. As we have seen in Chapter 2, identifying the key drivers of engagement will help you best understand the business priorities. Clearly any engagement strategy should be aligned to the organization's strategy.

I am not a believer that HR functions should develop their own visions. HR's role is to support the business in the management of its people, therefore its vision should be that of the organization. An employee engagement strategy should support and bolster the organizational vision, mission and business objectives.

THE PROCESS OF DEVELOPING A STRATEGY

To ensure that your employee engagement strategy is linked to business objectives, you should take the following steps in developing an employee engagement strategy:

▌ Develop a SWOT or priority matrix for the employee engagement survey (see Chapter 3 for examples).

▌ Outline the organization's vision, mission and values.

▌ Outline the organization's key objectives.

▌ Define the employee engagement strategy and how this supports the organization's vision, mission, values and key objectives.

▌ Set specific goals and measures of success for the employee engagement strategy.

▌ Describe the actions to be taken to achieve the goals, what will happen, when and where, and who will be responsible.

In the case of the optician retailer, the vision for the organization was 'to be the clear choice for customers and employees'. Its objectives centred on acquisition and growth. If the optician retailer was going to achieve its vision and objectives, it needed to build on its current strengths and develop a more people-focused strategy.

As we have already seen, each company's culture is unique. What might work in one business to drive engagement may well not work in another. Even in the same industry sector there will be variants in need. At Standard Charter Bank, for example, the introduction of a robust talent management system helped boost engagement levels, at Nationwide Building Society it was an emphasis on work–life balance.

To help group the drivers of engagement into a meaningful plan of action for you to address, I have developed the WIFI model of engagement. Like a wireless network, its make up is invisible to the eye but once connected it allows you to work efficiently and wherever you are. This state of 'flow' – the term used by the American Psychological Association to describe the state of mind in which people become completely involved and so immersed in an activity that they lose track of time – is when an employee is highly engaged. When the network is down the employee becomes quickly disengaged and disaffected.

THE WIFI MODEL

Like a network, the WIFI model of engagement is made up of some basic components that when brought together are very powerful. In my experience of best practice organizations there are four key elements that drive employee engagement:

- well-being;
- information;
- fairness;
- involvement.

Well-being

Feeling good about the organization and having the organization in turn care for you is a fundamental aspect of engagement. There are two facets to this component: external and internal. In the later chapter on well-being I explore the external aspects: corporate social responsibility (which is about how companies conduct their business and the impact that they have economically, socially, environmentally and in terms of human rights), and employer branding, which is about the external face that organizations project in order to attract and retain employees.

But well-being is far more than what we feel about the external face of the organization. Research indicates that engagement is more likely than not to be associated with a good work–life balance. HR policies such as flexible working hours and family-friendly policies go some way to generating a level of engagement.

Job design and structure, and having sufficient challenge in a job and sufficient resources to do the job well are equally important in helping employees feel fulfilled in their roles. Likewise, well-being encompasses equality and diversity policies that go beyond compliance with anti-discrimination legislation and can lead to greater levels of employee engagement.

A further aspect of this element is genuine care for the employee as expressed by their immediate line manager. Well-being is also underpinned by a set of organizational values that employees see to be aligned to the behaviour they also see others display.

Information

Having a clear vision of where the organization is going and what it wants to achieve and communicating this effectively is an essential element in binding employees together. Having clarity around organizational goals appears in many studies as essential in helping employees to know where they are going and why and how they fit into achieving those goals. The regularity and appropriateness of information at all levels is a key driver of engagement.

Fairness

Fairness can be seen in many aspects of the employee journey, starting with recruitment and selection. Hiring the right people for the right jobs is fundamental to ensuring that individuals begin their working life with your organization in the most positive way.

Fairness also manifests itself in the performance management process your business adopts. Being clear about what is expected of employees in their job and receiving regular and timely motivational and developmental feedback appear as key factors in all research on employee engagement.

Likewise, it has been established that it is important for employees to have a personal development plan. Ready access to training and development that meets individual needs has been proven to be important for many organizations in developing a culture of engagement. Research into employee engagement by BlessingsWhite demonstrated that career and talent management are important to many people.

Finally, businesses with high levels of employee engagement provide appropriate and fair reward and recognition.

Involvement

Organizations with high levels of employee engagement recognize that communication is a two-way process. They actively engage in conversation with their employees. According to a recent study by Watson Wyatt Worldwide, organizations with effective internal communications have a 19.4 per cent higher market premium and deliver 57 per cent higher shareholder return. The study also found a strong correlation between a company's communication and its employee engagement and retention levels. Firms that involve their employees effectively are 4.5 times more likely to report high levels of employee engagement than firms that communicate less effectively. They are also 20 per cent more likely to report lower turnover rates than their peers.

Involvement also manifests itself in the degree to which teamwork is actively promoted and encouraged.

The impact of the WIFI model

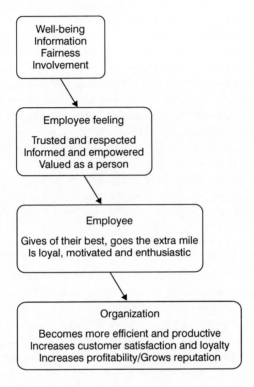

Figure 4.1 The impact of the WIFI model

Case studies using WIFI

The following are case studies outlining measures a variety of businesses have taken to improve their levels of employee engagement. Alongside each company's name I have indicated which aspects of the WIFI model have been addressed to improve the levels of engagement.

First Direct: well-being and fairness

At award winning telephone banking centre, First Direct, employee engagement scores improved over a two-year period owing in part to First Direct recognizing the key drivers of employee engagement for their business. In a call centre environment where attrition rates typically run at 20–25 per cent (and over 100 per cent in Indian call centres), First Direct's employee engagement survey identified that career development and leadership effectiveness were the two drivers for engagement.

The organization employs over 2,700 people in its two UK call centres in Leeds and Hamilton. The feedback from employees was that there was not a clear line of sight from a call centre agent to the CEO. First Direct created a leadership development programme to address this need. The company recognized the key role that team leaders and managers take in creating an environment where people give of their best. Other initiatives that have increased engagement scores include mentoring by senior managers of new call centre operators, job swapping, senior managers 'back to the floor' initiatives and job shadowing.

First Direct also provides a variety of packages to promote well-being, including a concierge service, ironing service, massage facility, hairdresser, gym and the largest on-site nursery in the United Kingdom. It has an attrition rate of just 14.2 per cent, compared with the national average of 25 per cent for call centres. The average length of employee stay is six years.

Hallmark: well-being, information, fairness and involvement

Hallmark is the renowned manufacturer of greetings cards and other greetings products. In the United Kingdom in the early 2000s the company went through a period of radical change including the merger of five companies. To help create a new company ethic the group MD reviewed the business's vision and values. A new vision 'Enriching lives and relationships' was developed together with a set of company values. These were communicated by the executive via a series of roadshows. At the same time, work began with the senior leadership team to build a high-performance team. This used the concept of emotional intelligence, based on Goleman's 1996 work, to create greater personal understanding in terms of self-awareness, interpersonal skills, stress management and emotional state. The concept was then rolled out with other senior leadership teams across the group. HR supported the change strategy by undertaking a number of initiatives that were aligned to the vision and values. These included:

▌ launching of family-friendly policies;

▌ flexible working;

▌ a new intranet site;

▌ online job applications;

▌ the implementation of an annual staff survey;

▌ management guides to HR practices;

- a bimonthly newsletter;

- cross-functional awareness sessions;

- career progression planning;

- a new appraisal system that includes the company values;

- development of internal trainers and an internal training calendar;

- creation of HR business partners.

The result of these initiatives has been a marked increase in employee engagement.

Microsoft: well-being and information

IT giant Microsoft has repeatedly won awards as an employer of choice and for 'best company to work for'. Unpopular in quarters for its technological omnipresence, it has won accolades for promoting work–life balance. Employees are encouraged to work flexibly and have laptops and broadband internet access at home. Other benefits include a crèche and family days when employees are encouraged to bring their children to work; subsidised restaurants and gym membership, free private healthcare as well as well-man and well-woman clinics. If an employee would like to undertake an activity on behalf of a charity, Microsoft will match the financial contribution like for like.

Microsoft has low levels of attrition (6 per cent on the sales and marketing side in the United Kingdom and 2 per cent on the technical side, for example). The organization attributes this to its 'great company' strategy. A central platform of this is to ensure that staff understand what Microsoft is, where it is going and what its strategies mean at grass-roots level. Openness is a recurrent theme that manifests itself in one-level sign off for expenses and purchases for example, and regular updates and online information.

National Australia Group: well-being, information, fairness and involvement

National Australia Group Europe (NAGE) has made a remarkable increase in its levels of employee engagement to win the accolade of best contact centre (with 250 plus seats) in the world. With annual attrition rates at 65 per cent the company recognized that it needed to undertake radical change to make it world class. At one point the company was training new staff faster than it could recruit.

The business introduced a number of initiatives to improve levels of employee engagement. First, a leadership development programme to improve the skills, knowledge and behaviours of managers was introduced. At the same time a new measurement process, called 'Scores on the board', was introduced. This measures performance against a set of key indicators: engaged staff, satisfied customers, increased productivity and increased revenue. It is the basis of the improvement initiative and is used by managers every week as part of one-to-one discussions. The idea is to encourage individuals to view the organization as their own business. Each team analyses employee and customer feedback and devises their own plan of action to address any gaps. The peer review of goals that are related to aspects of work within employees' control has helped created an environment of empowerment. In addition to the leadership development programme and the setting of new performance measures, the HR department did a considerable amount of work to develop well-being and career development programmes. For example, the centre has provided additional product knowledge and skills training as well as ensuring that everyone has a personal development plan.

During the course of the year's programme, levels of team motivation, self-management, engagement and performance have increased. In 12 months attrition plummeted from 65 per cent to less than 40 per cent and absences from 12 per cent to under 5 per cent.

Key learning points

▎ The drivers of employee engagement will be different for each organization.

▎ They will consist of different combinations of activities to promote WIFI.

▎ Unless you know what the key drivers are it will be difficult to bring about any sustained change in engagement scores.

USING WIFI IN YOUR ORGANIZATION

To give you a sense of where your business needs to improve, I have cross-referenced the example survey that appears in Chapter 2 to the WIFI model. You can use this or a version of this survey across your organization. Alternatively, I suggest that you complete the survey yourself and ask a small sample of people from your organization to do so too anonymously.

Questions are scored by participants indicating agreement on a scale of 1 to 10 to each one, where 1 and 2 indicates disagree very strongly through to 9 or 10 indicating very strong agreement. There are no right or wrongs, honest opinions count. Analyse your scores using the section 'How to interpret your score'. You results will provide a 'dip-stick' of what you do well and where potential improvements can be made. Make sure that you follow this up with more robust research to verify your evidence.

Section 1: Relates to fairness

The organization recruits and selects the right people to the right jobs.

Your score out of 10: _____

I receive appropriate training and development to help me do my job well.

Your score out of 10: _____

I have a personal development plan that helps me grow and develop my career.

Your score out of 10: _____

I have ample opportunity to develop my skills, knowledge and behaviours.

Your score out of 10: _____

I am given the appropriate level of authority to do a good job.

Your score out of 10: _____

I am satisfied with the opportunities there are to develop my career.

Your score out of 10: _____

The organization recognizes and develops people's talents.

Your score out of 10: _____

I receive appropriate pay and benefits for the job that I do.

Your score out of 10: _____

In the past month I have received praise and recognition for a job well done.

Your score out of 10: _____

My manager reviews my performance with me on a one-to-one basis at least once every six months.

Your score out of 10: _____

Total score: Fairness _____

Section 2: Relates to involvement

My immediate line manager makes me feel my contributions are valued.

Your score out of 10: _____

I feel appropriately involved in decision making.

Your score out of 10: _____

I am able to voice my views to my manager.

Your score out of 10: _____

My manager listens and acts on my views.

Your score out of 10: _____

Managers in this organization encourage two-way communication that promotes open and honest dialogue and understanding.

Your score out of 10: _____

Teamwork is encouraged in my work unit/department.

Your score out of 10: _____

The organization promotes internal cooperation.

Your score out of 10: _____

I feel part of a family working for this organization.

Your score out of 10: _____

I trust my colleagues to do a good job.

Your score out of 10: _____

I am encouraged to come up with new ways of doing things.

Your score out of 10: _____

Total score: Involvement _____

Section 3: Relates to well-being

My immediate line manager cares for me as a person.

Your score out of 10: _____

This organization makes an effective contribution to the community.

Your score out of 10: _____

This organization promotes equal opportunities.

Your score out of 10: _____

I am not overloaded with work to do.

Your score out of 10: _____

I have appropriately stimulating and challenging work.

Your score out of 10: _____

The organization promotes the health and well-being of employees.

Your score out of 10: _____

I am happy with my work–life balance.

Your score out of 10: _____

The organization has appropriate family-friendly policies.

Your score out of 10: _____

I have the appropriate resources to do my job well.

Your score out of 10: _____

I can relate to the values of this organization.

Your score out of 10: _____

Total score: Well-being _____

Section 4: Information

Communication across the organization is effective.

Your score out of 10: _____

The goals of this organization are clear.

Your score out of 10: _____

I receive timely information to help me do my job well.

Your score out of 10: _____

I have trust in the leaders of this organization.

Your score out of 10: _____

I have a clear understanding of the vision of this organization.

Your score out of 10: _____

The job that I do adds value to the organization.

Your score out of 10: _____

I am clear what is expected of me in my role.

Your score out of 10: _____

Senior managers lead by example.

Your score out of 10: _____

I am informed at appropriate intervals about what our customers think about us.

Your score out of 10: _____

I am aware of the values of the organization.

Your score out of 10: _____

Total score: Involvement: _____

Section 5: Indicators of the degree of engagement

I am proud to work for this organization.

Your score out of 10: _____

I would recommend this organization to others as a good place to work.

Your score out of 10: _____

I care about the future of this organization.

Your score out of 10: _____

I would recommend to my friends and family that they do business with this organization.

Your score out of 10: _____

I am willing to go the extra mile on behalf of the organization.

Your score out of 10: _____

Total score: Degree of engagement: _____

You can also download an electronic copy of this diagnostic tool by visiting our website: www.thestairway.co.uk.

HOW TO INTERPRET YOUR SCORE

Scores for the four WIFI sections

For each question our experience is that the average score is 7 out of 10. So when you total each of the first four sections: well-being, information, fairness and involvement, each person's individual scores (or the average scores of all the questionnaires) will indicate the following for each section:

▍ 75 and over. This score would indicate a high degree of engagement in this element.

▍ 55–74. This score would indicate an average degree of engagement in this aspect of WIFI.

▍ 1–54. This score would indicate a low degree of engagement in this aspect of WIFI.

Scores for the indicators of the degree of employee engagement

For section 5: Indicators of the degree of engagement, scores will predict the following:

▍ 32 and over. This score would indicate a high degree of engagement.

▍ 22–31. This score would indicate an average degree of engagement.

▍ 1–21. This score would indicate a low degree of engagement.

In addition, look at the lowest scoring aspects of each of the WIFI sections and the three lowest scoring items for the whole questionnaire. This should give you an indication of the key areas for improvement.

Overall score

▍ If the overall score for all five sections is 332 or above, this indicates an above average degree of engagement.

▍ Looking at all five sections of the survey, if the overall score is between 242 and 331, this indicates an average degree of engagement.

▌ If the overall score for all five sections of the survey is between 5 and 241, this indicates a lower than average degree of engagement.

Key learning points

▌ Remember to check via focus groups and one-to-one interviews that the results of the survey do indicate the correct key drivers of employee engagement.

▌ Do not expect that improving one aspect of WIFI alone will bring about dramatic changes in engagement scores. As the case studies demonstrate, it is often the combination of improvements in different aspects of the four elements of WIFI that bring about change.

TRANSFORMATIONAL CHANGE

The optician retailer with whom I worked identified from the WIFI model that it needed to make improvements in some aspects of well-being, information, fairness and particularly in many aspects of involvement. The organization recognized that these changes could not be made overnight.

Remember that creating true employee engagement is a cultural issue. It often involves breaking ingrained patterns of working. To embed employee engagement as a real business change requires commitment to building an integrated strategy that aligns engagement improvement areas with business priorities. It needs sponsorship from the top of the organization and consistent monitoring and commitment to ensure that the improvement actions are on track.

Long-term improvements in employee engagement need to be endorsed by the leadership team of your organization. They need to be part of an overall strategy of HCM.

John Kotter, Harvard Business School Professor of Leadership cites why many improvement initiatives fail:

▌ allowing too much complacency;

▌ failing to create a sufficiently powerful guiding coalition;

▌ underestimating the power of vision;

▌ failing to create short-term wins;

▌ neglecting to anchor changes firmly in the corporate culture.

These reasons apply equally to the introduction of employee engagement strategies as to any other change. Organizations that are successful in implementing employee engagement programmes do so by:

▍ analysing the organization and its readiness for change;

▍ creating a shared vision and common direction;

▍ demonstrating strong leadership;

▍ creating a sense of urgency;

▍ developing a participative implementation process;

▍ communicating and involving people;

▍ supporting and recognizing success.

I recommend that you use these as guiding principles when you set out to improve your levels of engagement.

CREATING AN EMPLOYEE ENGAGEMENT PROGRAMME

The results of the employee engagement survey proved a wake-up call for the high street optician retailer. The HR director recognized that the journey to higher levels of engagement would probably take a two- to three-year period and that there should be agreed milestones on the way. The involvement of people from across the business in a series of working parties was critical to the success of the process, as undoubtedly was the support from the leadership team.

Effectively, the HR director saw the journey to greater engagement as a programme involving a series of discreet projects. An employee engagement programme normally consists of a set of coordinated and controlled projects that are undertaken to implement business change.

WORK BREAKDOWN STRUCTURE

A starting point therefore for developing an employee engagement programme is to identify the likely work breakdown structure. One way of doing this is to draw a diagram that indicates the programme's different activities in a top–down format showing large work packages and smaller packages down to a size suitable for discrete projects. It is useful because people can see at a glance how much work is needed and how it might be organised.

Once you have decided on the work breakdown structure for the programme you can decide the structure and make-up of the individual projects. When creating project teams to implement improvements in employee engagement, consider the common elements of successful programmes and ensure that you use these guidelines to set up your programme.

The Institute of Project Management in the United Kingdom has identified a number of variables that lead to successful programme implementation. These are (in order of importance):

1. The involvement of the customer, or end-user

2. The support of senior management

3. A clear statement of requirements (including objectives, deliverables and outputs, and business objectives)

4. Proper, considered planning

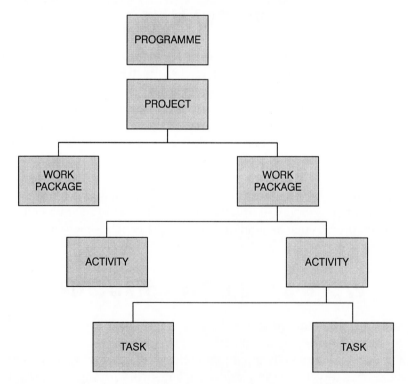

Figure 4.2 Example of work breakdown structure

5. Realistic expectations and timescales

6. Competent, focused project members

7. Effective, circular communication.

In practice this means that to be successful you need to adopt a structured approach to the employee engagement programme. This involves thorough and robust planning, securing stakeholder ownership, defining and agreeing expectations, creating and managing project teams, monitoring and controlling progress against the plan, anticipating or overcoming blockages, learning from mistakes and celebrating success.

FOUR STAGES OF AN EMPLOYEE ENGAGEMENT PROGRAMME

The next section summarizes the four stages of creating an employee engagement programme.

Defining the programme

Make sure that you have a programme sponsor. Agree the vision of the programme. Use the WIFI model to define what needs to happen, the number and types of projects in the programme, exactly what they will achieve and by when. Check that you have the resources and the skills you need.

Planning

Allocate resources – time, people and materials – to each project and to the programme working party. Establish a project leader for each team and project team members. If necessary, arrange for any training or briefing. Agree roles and responsibilities (who will do what). Set milestones. Agree the reporting mechanism for each project with the programme management team.

Implementing and monitoring

Ensure that each project has a 30-day, 60-day and 90-day plan so that everyone is clear what needs to be achieved and by when. As a rule of thumb if changes, no matter how small, are not implemented for each project within 90 days, the project is not likely to gain acceptance from key stakeholders. Monitor the progress of each project. Make sure that everyone is informed of progress, particularly where there are interdependencies between projects. Encourage an atmosphere where problems are discussed openly. Don't blame people for mistakes – try to correct them and continue the project.

Evaluate the process

When each project is complete, evaluate the short-, medium- and long-term benefits. Make sure that people at all levels understand the benefits and lessons learned. Share these with other project team members involved in the programme.

DEFINING ROLES AND RESPONSIBILITIES

If you are setting up a programme or project, one of the first tasks is to define the roles and responsibilities of the people involved. These are the sponsor, the project or programme manager and the project team members. There are four aspects of the programme or project that need to be considered: how to organize the programme or project, how to achieve the tasks, how to manage the people involved and the personal qualities that are needed. Figure 4.3 provides a checklist for programme or project member roles. Use this to ensure that you have clarity and that you have the right people represented on your project team.

THE PROJECT SCOPING PROCESS

Once you have established the programme working party and identified the different projects that link to the WIFI model, it is helpful for the project team members of each project to agree the scope of the project. This can then be ratified by the programme management team.

You may have your own internal project initiation documents, but for those who don't, it is essential that all project team members agree and document the following aspects of the project:

Organizing the programme or project

SPONSOR	PROJECT MANAGER	TEAM MEMBER
Takes a helicopter view	Communicates vision and goals	Understands the big picture
Ensures strategic fit	Identifies/involves stakeholders	Has commercial/business awareness
Is customer focused	Has commercial/business awareness	
Works across boundaries	Tackles issues/problems	
Champions change	Is politically sensitive	
Manages expectations		
Is accountable		

Achieving the programme or project tasks

SPONSOR	PROJECT MANAGER	TEAM MEMBER
Identifies user need	Sets and agrees goals	Is objective, critical
Resolves issues	Produces schedules	Is innovative and proactive
Demonstrates business acumen	Establishes budgets	Uses judgement and makes decisions
Monitors project quality, timescales, budgets	Estimates effort	Is conscious of detail
	Analyses risks	Gathers and analyses data
	Establishes, organizes and motivates the team	Is a team player
	Is involved in data handling	
	Is able to multitask	

Figure 4.3 Programme or project member roles

Programme or project organization – people skills needed

SPONSOR	PROJECT MANAGER	TEAM MEMBER
Influences, persuades, sells	Champions and defends the team	Challenges/supports
Uses networks and the organization's politics well	Manages conflict	Co-coaches
Motivates the project leader and the team	Motivates/leads	Works well as part of a team
	Coaches	
	Manages performance	
	Delegates	

Programme or project organization – personal skills needed

SPONSOR	PROJECT MANAGER	TEAM MEMBER
Uses judgement, makes decisions	Is a good communicator	Is a good communicator
Is resilient	Has feedback skills	Is open minded
Is determined	Has tenacity/focus	Has energy/commitment
Is a risk taker	Has confidence/energy	Is assertive
Is prepared to take an independent stand	Is assertive	
Shows drive and commitment	Has integrity	

Figure 4.3 *continued*

▌ Background:

- What is the justification for the project, what is this based on and what would the perceived benefits be?

- Who are the customers or stakeholders in the project?

▌ Objectives:

- What do you want the project to achieve in SMART terms?

- Which key issues will the project address or resolve?

- How does the project fit in with your strategic aims?

▌ Deliverables:

- What are the deliverables or outputs for this project?

▌ Within the project's scope:

- What are the boundaries or parameters of this project? Where do these boundaries or parameters cross with other projects?

▌ Outside the project's scope:

- What are you not looking at including in this project?

▌ Assumptions:

- What assumptions are you making about this project? (eg having the current project team as a resource for the length of the project)

▌ Constraints:

- What are the constraints of this project? (eg budgetary constraints)

▌ Anticipated phases:

- What are the different phases of delivery?

▌ Timescale:

- Estimate timescales for each phase.

▌ Estimated effort:

- How many people will be needed to implement the project and for how long?

▌ Risks and mitigating actions:

- What are the risks involved in the project?

- What is the probability of them occurring – high, medium or low?

- What is the likely impact?

- What mitigating action can you take to lower the probability of risks and their impact?

▌ Contacts:

- Who is the project manager and the project sponsor and what are their contact details?

- Who are the project team members and what are their contact details?

▌ Authorizations:

– Who has the authority to make decisions and sign off the project? (eg the project sponsor)

PLANNING RESOURCES

A useful way of ensuring that all programme and project team members know what needs to happen and who is responsible is to prepare a RACI chart. This outlines the key activities, timescales, who is responsible, who is accountable, who to consult and who to inform about each activity.

Figure 4.4 is an example RACI chart. Details about the chart's column headings are given below:

▌ Responsible = 'Doer'. This means individuals who perform an activity – they are responsible for action or implementation. The accountable person defines the degree of responsibility. Responsibilities can be shared.

▌ Accountable = 'The buck stops here'. This is the individual who is ultimately accountable, including saying yes or no, having the power of veto. Only one accountable person can be assigned to an activity or decision.

▌ Consult = 'In the loop'. Here list the individuals who need to be consulted prior to a decision or action being taken. Two-way communication is vital in all forms of consultation.

▌ Inform = 'For your information'. This column will include all individuals who need to be informed after a decision or action is taken. One-way communication is sufficient for this.

If you use a RACI chart, remember to get buy-in to it by including all project team members in its completion.

WORKING WELL AS A PROJECT TEAM

One of the factors that determines the success of your programme will be the extent to which you and your fellow project team members work well together as a team. Therefore, if you are leading the programme or project it can be helpful to review this aspect, not just how well you are achieving the tasks.

Task description	Responsible	Accountable	Consult	Inform

Figure 4.4 Example of a RACI chart

When you look at the following roles and responsibilities of the programme leader, you will see that the challenge in championing a programme of employee engagement is not just in project managing the tasks but also in leading and managing the team. The programme leader:

- sets and agrees clear goals;

- produces schedules;

- establishes budgets;

- estimates resources;

- analyses risks and makes contingencies;

- communicates the vision;

- structures the team and establishes roles;

- identifies individual and team needs;

- agrees clear responsibilities and accountabilities;

- leads and manages meetings effectively;

- creates an open climate (through support and challenge);

- confronts and resolves issues;

- monitors progress and holds regular reviews;

- reviews individual and team performance;

- recognizes and rewards effective contribution;

- coaches where appropriate;

- gives and seeks feedback;

- listens and responds;

- demonstrates effective influencing and negotiation skills;

- works across boundaries;

- communicates effectively to all involved;

- transfers the learning;

- champions and defends the team.

Checklist

Which of the four elements of WIFI need to be improved in your organization?

List which aspects of WIFI need to be improved for your organization.

Develop a work breakdown structure to show the activities that need to be undertaken.

Whose buy-in do you need to gain to make these improvements happen?

What key areas of the business need to represented on a programme or project team?

This chapter has described how to develop a strategy for employee engagement. It has introduced a model of employee engagement called WIFI, which stands for well-being, involvement, fairness and information. Depending on the results of your employee engagement survey, you may need to improve different aspects of WIFI to increase levels of engagement. This chapter has looked at how best to set up a programme or project to implement improvements in levels of employee engagement. The subsequent chapters provide detail of activities you can consider to improve engagement levels in the areas of well-being, involvement, fairness and information. The next chapter focuses on well-being.

5

Well-being

This chapter is the start of four chapters on the different aspects of the WIFI model. It provides practical pointers and best practice examples to help you develop a plan of action to make improvements if required in each of the areas. This chapter looks at the importance of well-being to employees' levels of engagement. It demonstrates that well-being is not just about the welfare of the workforce. It is also about how employees perceive the employer brand and what it stands for. This chapter starts by taking a closer look at employee motivation and the issue of spirituality, which is growing in importance in Western economies and will also impact emerging economies. The second part of the chapter focuses on employee welfare and work–life balance.

WHAT IS WELL-BEING?

As you may remember from previous chapters, the optician retail chain had recently grown through acquisition of a smaller group of similar companies. The results of the optician retailer's employee engagement survey showed a divergence in views between employees of the two former companies. The majority of employees that had worked for the company that has been acquired (let's call it company B), were critical of the new organization and its stance towards customer service. They expressed feelings of disassociation with the new organization and when asked preferred to say both internally and externally that they were employed by company B rather than the new firm. In fact many of the compensation and benefits that they were offered by the new organization were better than those of their previous company. However, their feelings and perception of the new company and what it stood for were far from positive.

Well-being in this context has two aspects: how the company is perceived externally and how well employees are treated internally.

Businesses often espouse a set of values that purport to genuinely care for their employees, but to what extent do they do this in practice? A fundamental aspect of engagement is how the employee feels about the employer. Does the member of staff feel proud to work for the organization? Do they believe that the business cares for them as an individual? What other people think about the organization also shapes employees' sense of well-being. For example, how corporately responsible is the organization? Does it care about the community in which it operates? Does it conduct its business in an ethical and moral fashion? How does it present itself as a brand to potential recruits?

Family-friendly policies and the degree to which the organization promotes a work-life balance also foster a sense of well-being. Other policies such as those truly promoting equality and diversity are important too.

Other issues that affect the way that the individual feels about their employer are job design and structure. If a job is boring or repetitive and lacks challenge, or if an employee has insufficient resources to do their job well, they are hardly likely to feel fulfilled in their role.

One of the main aspects of well-being is also an intangible one – the feeling that individuals have that their direct line manager genuinely cares about them as a person.

When well-being at work is poor not only will an organization suffer from low levels of employee engagement but this will manifest itself in working days lost through sickness and injury. In the United Kingdom the Confederation of British Industry puts the total number of days lost through ill health and injury at 35 million in 2006 at a cost of £12 billion. It estimates that 3–5 per cent of the UK workforce on any one day may be away from work. A further 25–30 per cent are at work but performing suboptimally because of ill health.

MOTIVATION

Well-being is as much a state of mind as it is a physical characteristic. It is fundamental to the degree to which employees feel motivated to give discretionary effort. To help best understand well-being, therefore, we need to better understand beliefs about motivation.

There are many theories and insights that management psychologists and behaviouralists have come up with about human motivation. Certainly this is a complex area in terms of human energy and behaviour. What most specialists agree, however, is that:

▌ Motivation comes from within; it is drawn out of individuals, not imposed on them.

▌ Motivation is multi-dimensional and there is no single universal answer about what motivation is, true for all time and all people.

▌ Some things motivate and encourage extra effort; others only cause dissatisfaction by their absence.

▌ Clear goals are an aid to motivation: they enable individuals to know what to aim for, and feedback gives an energizing sense of progress.

▌ Increasingly, 'carrots' are seen as generally more effective to foster sustained motivation than 'sticks'.

To foster long-term, sustained motivation, recent thought is that managers must inspire employees to draw their motivation from inside rather than rely on external factors such as pay.

One of the more recent theorists on motivation, Spitzer, makes interesting points in relation to employee engagement. Spitzer (1995) outlines eight fundamental needs that motivate employees in the long term and which are shared to varying degrees by us all. These are:

▌ Desire for activity. People want to be active and involved. In their personal lives most people avoid boredom and monotony. Yet at work employees are expected to accept boring, repetitive, monotonous jobs without complaint.

▌ Desire for ownership. Owning things makes people feel better about themselves. 'Psychological' ownership is even more important than 'physical' ownership. Employees want to psychologically own their work. They want input into their work and want to feel responsible for their jobs.

▌ Desire for power. People want to control their destiny. They don't want to feel powerless over external forces shaping their lives. With fewer top-down, control organizations more and more employees are demanding their freedom back.

▌ Desire for affiliation. People are social creatures. They like to interact and socialize with one another, though the degree of sociability will vary. Social support and helping relationships are among the many benefits provided by work.

▌ Desire for competence. This is the core of self-esteem. People welcome opportunities to feel more competent. Work can provide these opportunities.

▌ Desire for achievement. It is important for people to succeed at something. Under the right conditions, employees will be willing to work hard and overcome obstacles to achieve a goal.

▌ Desire for recognition. People want to feel appreciated by others and be positively recognized for their efforts. Recognition is a powerful force which has the capability to unleash energy and motivation.

▌ Desire for meaning. People want a reason for doing something. They want reassurance that their efforts, however small, are making a difference.

Spitzer advocates that the manager finds out which of these eight desires the individual most wishes to satisfy and then facilitate ways of helping the employee achieve these desires.

AFFILIATION AND MEANING

In terms of well-being, factors that Spitzer identifies for affiliation and meaning are important in relation to the external face of the organization as well as how people are treated internally. Employees want to be affiliated with organizations that they can be proud of. In addition, they are increasingly looking for meaningful work that makes a difference to communities and society as a whole. Businesses today have three key tools to use in appealing to this aspect of employee well-being:

▌ corporate social responsibility;

▌ employer branding;

▌ organizational values.

CORPORATE SOCIAL RESPONSIBILITY (CSR)

Against a backdrop of corporate scandals such as the Enron scandal in the United States, employees are increasingly questioning the ethical stance of their organization and the contribution that businesses make beyond their immediate business environment. Many organizations now look to put back into society a contribution that involves helping the wider community or environment.

As already stated, CSR refers to how companies conduct their business and the impact that they have economically, socially, environmentally and in terms of human rights. Look at most well-known businesses and you will probably find that they have some form of CSR programme. From accountants KPMG that sends its partners in to schools to help with literacy classes, to airline Southwest Airlines that provides volunteers from its workforce to clean up graffiti in run-down areas, there is a wide range of activities that businesses can and do undertake.

Nowadays most organizations recognize the business advantages of CSR. Successful CSR can bring benefits such as a helping create a distinct position in your marketplace and building credibility and trust with current and potential customers, and with employees. It can help significantly to paint a good image of the organization when it comes to recruitment, engagement and retention of employees.

The effect of CSR on employee engagement?

Cynically people may see corporate social responsibility as just another way of attracting good candidates to an organization and also to establish a 'feel good' factor for existing employees. But organizations that do CSR well genuinely have a commitment to altruistic causes. When done well, engaging in CSR can also bring financial pay-offs. A 2006 study done at the University of Chicago by Professor Curtis Verschoor and published in *Management Accounting* found that companies with a defined corporate commitment to ethical principles do better financially than companies that do not make ethics a key management component. This is the same for many multinational (and smaller) companies now – they need to be *seen* to be good, green and/or ethical. Consumers and employees are increasingly aware and increasingly critical.

Case studies

Coca-Cola

Nothing symbolizes globalization quite as powerfully as Coca-Cola. It established a presence in Africa as early as 1928 and the company's growth across the continent accelerated from the 1960s as African countries gained their independence. Today, Coca-Cola has operations in all 56 African countries, with 40 bottling firms operating 170 plants under licence as part of its 'franchise' system. This makes it Africa's largest private-sector employer, with over 60,000 employees in the Coca-Cola system.

Coca-Cola has embraced CSR in Africa via its support of HIV/AIDS workplace policies. These include confidential screening and antiretroviral provision for workers and their immediate families. Coca-Cola puts in excess of 1 per cent (to date, over US$140 million) of its profits before tax into its corporate social responsibility programmes.

Lucent Technologies

Since 1999 involving employees in community service has been an integral part of Lucent Technologies' employee engagement strategy. In India, for example, the company has formed an alliance with several NGOs to bring computer-assisted learning modules to schools and communities. In addition, Lucent employees act as guest lecturers at schools and mentor disabled youth in Bangalore. In Mexico employees have trained over 1,200 teachers in innovative science teaching methods. In Russia the company sponsored a competition to encourage young people to develop innovative information technology products. Lucent holds 'Global Days of Caring' where every year for a week or more local offices commit to support local philanthropies.

Timberland

The Timberland Company, a manufacturer and retailer of footwear, outdoor apparel and accessories, committed itself to instituting and communicating a core set of values to its employees, stockholders and consumers. One of its core beliefs emphasized community service. Central to this commitment was an alliance with the national youth community service organization, City Year. Employees from throughout the organization are encouraged to work on a voluntary basis with the charity. They are given paid leave to do so.

Co-operative Society

The Co-operative Society is one of the United Kingdom's oldest socially conscious communities. Its employees are mainly employed in the retail arena in shops and convenience stores across the country. A non-profit making organization, each year it donates a percentage of its surplus to benefit local community projects. In addition each year the Society asks its employees to vote for the charity that it should support throughout the year. Once employees have made a selection, it helps organize events and activities throughout the business to enable employees to raise money for the chosen charity. It matches the money raised by employees on a like-for-like basis.

Key learning points

▌ If your organization undertakes CSR, involve employees in the selection of the activities.

▌ Make sure that the CSR programme is relevant to your business area, your community and employee interests.

▌ Ensure that your CSR programme is not a corporate image management exercise or other activity aimed predominantly at business benefits.

Figure 5.1 is a checklist that will help you develop a successful CSR strategy.

Rate your organization against each criterion in Figure 5.1. Identify what aspects of your strategy need to be addressed. Potentially if many aspects of your strategy need to be addressed, it would be advisable to establish a project team to develop this further. Ultimately, depending on the size of your business, full-time dedicated resources may be needed for this area.

THE EMPLOYER BRAND

A further means of increasing employees' sense of well-being is by building a successful employer brand. An effective employer brand is a set of attributes and qualities that make an organization attractive and distinctive to potential and existing employees. A recent Job Index Survey shows that the companies that attract and retain high fliers are those with the best employer brands – but what is an employer brand?

	In place	Needs to be addressed
The principles of our CSR strategy are clear		
Our CSR strategy is aligned to our corporate strategy		
Our CSR strategy links to our corporate values		
We have consulted our external and internal stakeholders to ensure that the CSR strategy is appropriate		
Our senior management team actively supports our CSR strategy		
The sponsor of our CSR strategy is a member of the senior management team		
Our CSR strategy is aligned to our HR policies and practices		
We have training in place to support our CSR strategy		
We have effective measures in place to evaluate our CSR strategy		
We have clearly communicated the aims and objectives of our CSR policy		

Figure 5.1   Checklist for the development of a successful CSR strategy

The outward face of the brand

In recent years HR professionals have become more aware of the power of the brand to attract and retain talented employees. David Dell, former Research Director of The Conference Board's Capabilities Management and Human Resources Strategies Area said on their website:

> The challenge to employers is not only to make potential employees aware of the company as a good place to work and bring the best applicants successfully through the recruitment and hiring process, but to retain them and ensure their understanding of the company's goals and commitment to them. Companies have found employer branding programmes provide a real edge in competing for talent.

Many organizations are now working hard to promote their brand as a 'great place to work'. Yet this is against a climate where trust and recognition of the brand is in decline. A report conducted by researchers in 31 countries via face-to-face interviews with 31,000 people between the ages of 13 and 65 found that recognition of global brands in general is on the decline; and that the popularity and consumption of both US and non-US brands has declined for the first time since the research programme began in 1998.

The survey found that the number of consumers who 'trust' Coca-Cola fell from 55 per cent to 52 per cent, McDonald's from 36 per cent to 33 per cent, Nike from 56 per cent to 53 per cent and Microsoft from 45 per cent to 39 per cent between 2002 and 2005. Likewise, when asked about brands associated with 'honesty' the same companies fell a few percentage points. So which organizations have the best reputation? The Reputation Institute in the United States undertakes annual global surveys investigating which companies have the best reputation among employees and customers. The 2007 report found the top three companies with the best reputations to be the Swedish toy company Lego, home furnishing company Ikea and Italian food manufacturer Barilla.

Living the brand

Living the brand seems to come naturally to some organizations, though in fact it involves close attention to strategy and management. Airline Virgin Atlantic aims to deliver exceptional customer service and comes across as a fun and informal place to work. Financial services organization First Direct has an enviable reputation among customers and employees. JP MorganChase promotes itself to both customers and potential employees under the concept of leadership: 'One firm, one team, be a leader.'

Ultimately employer branding is about communicating the statement: 'We're an outstanding company and a good place to work.' Employees will be able to judge how true this is, and if they believe in the brand of their company they will sell that brand to potential customers and recruits.

Employer branding has been defined as 'the company's image as seen through the eyes of its employees and potential hires'. As the search for high-quality candidates for jobs becomes increasingly difficult, companies are now more conscious of the brand image they project and the need to be seen as 'the employer of choice'. There are several well-known examples, such as Agilent Technologies and the financial services organization Abbey, that show that where a coherent external message is developed about the brand it can help in attracting and retaining good candidates to the business. The treatment of employees and the quality of products and services are highest in jobsearchers' perceptions of the company they want to work for rather than financial success.

Strong employer brands such as Goldman Sachs International, which won the *Sunday Times* 2007 'Best Companies to Work For' award develop a distinctive value proposition. A strong employer brand sets out clearly what the organization stands for, what it offers employees and what it requires as an employer.

Increasingly, organizations recognize the importance of their brand. Some businesses are adopting dedicated employer branding efforts aimed at aligning employees with their organization's vision and values. Others are pursuing this goal as one element of broader corporate branding strategies. People are now realizing that to relegate *branding* to an advertising agency or the marketing department is only one piece of the jigsaw. The larger part of *branding* is how an organization delivers on its promise and this really differentiates it from the rest of the marketplace. And the people who deliver on that promise are employees. As a result, making sure that they understand and can deliver the brand to customers is vital – especially for companies in service industries, where the relationship between employees and customers is essentially the product the company sells.

Anecdotal evidence points to a growing trend for job seekers to look for work that is meaningful. They want to work for a company that reflects their own ideals and aspirations, so employer branding – the reputation of a company – is a vital element of the employment package. For example, it is reported that one of the overriding reasons why so many UK graduates are now opting to work for the public sector is that they feel that there is more heart and soul in the NHS, in teaching or in local government than there is in private enterprise. According to statistics, public sector organizations have never been as popular with graduates as they are today. The number of job applications that well-known charities report far outweighs the number of positions available and often candidates are over-qualified for the posts advertised.

Corporate entities with high moral principles such as Fairtrade, which has grown exponentially year on year, and Cafédirect, have experienced an increase in interest in them as an employer. 'Our vision is all about building social justice through trade. It runs through this organization like its bloodstream. Our DNA is embedded in ethics and values and is not something that can be assumed and then discarded', says Penny Newman, chief executive of Cafédirect, which is the United Kingdom's largest Fairtrade-accredited hot drinks organization. So the social impact of the organization on both society at large and the environment have grown in importance.

In non-Western economies employer branding has become equally as important as in the West. In China, for example, the current labour force is centred on three principle cities: Beijing, Guanghzou and Shanghai. Here salaries are relatively high and there is strong GDP growth. However, as the expected 150 million rural workers migrate to the city, it is expected that second- and third-tier cities will grow in prominence. Analysts predict that the growth of other centres will put increasing pressure on finding and keeping talent; the employer brand will therefore become more important. Already, for example, demand is growing for better corporate governance and transparency.

The key to creating a strong employer brand is to ensure that employees become 'brand ambassadors'. The strength of an employer brand can be adversely affected by any incongruence between the outward brand identity and employees' perception of the reality of the brand and the brand's reputation.

Research in 2006 by Hewitt Associates into staff at 1,200 global companies found that the top three reasons graduates join a company were the perception that the job would be fun, stability of employment and that the organization cared about employees. When the same survey was repeated once graduates started employment, their impressions of organizations had changed, with many citing they were demanding, under-resourced and not caring of employees.

Case studies

These case studies, giving examples of what to do and what not to do, come from the same sector: airlines.

easyJet is a low-cost airline that has a successful track record in Europe. Its workforce has grown to nearly 2,000 people since its inception in 1995. The brand values are that all members of staff are part of one big family, that they are unique and that the organization is fun. In order that the positive image of the brand be maintained, easyJet set about promoting the 'orangeness' of the brand (its brand logo is orange). To encourage employees to share the success of the airline they are offered bonuses and share plans, there is free food and drink on a Friday for all employees and free flights to new airline destinations for all staff. The company defines 'orangeness' as 'being up for it', 'passionate', 'sharp' and 'mad about cost'. Its employer brand reflects and mirrors its external brand.

A classical failure of external branding is United Airline's 'United Rising' campaign. This was created in the late 1990s to attract business flyers and to attract new recruits to the organization. From a customer perspective it promised attractive benefits, such as more leg room and better communications links. The problem was that the organization was completely unprepared to deliver on these promises. The operation was a highly unionized environment. At the same time that the business was beginning an external brand campaign, flight attendants were in dispute with the company about wage rises. There were low levels of engagement with the company. This manifested itself in a high degree of cynicism and resistance to the branding campaign.

Taking another example, this time from personal experience, one large global organization with whom I work projects an enviable reputation as an employer of choice, renowned for its customer focus. In reality when new recruits join, they find a highly bureaucratic and process-driven organization that is sales rather than customer focused. This leads to high levels of attrition, especially in the first three months.

Key learning points

▎ If you develop an employer branding campaign, make sure that your key external messages are congruent with what happens in the organization.

▎ Be honest in stating what employees can expect when working with you.

BRAND AND ORGANIZATIONAL VALUES

A less tangible aspect of well-being is the degree to which the espoused organizational or brand values are aligned with the behaviours people see in the workplace.

I have personally come across many businesses today that aim to increase employees' level of commitment and energy towards the organization by developing a set of values that should underpin the way that the company goes about its business. In essence, organizational values epitomize what the company and its brand stands for. For example, at retail financial services company Barclay's Bank, organizational values include professionalism and experience.

Why does having clearly defined organizational values increase engagement levels? On many levels being explicit about what the company stands for and what is important in the way that it works appeals to Spitzer's motivational desire outlines of giving 'meaning' to work. It is about connecting on an almost spiritual basis with the organization.

The term 'spiritual intelligence' was first coined by Zohar, who observed that in these rapidly changing times, values act as personal anchors which help people find meaning in their contribution at work. She identified that successful people have clearly thought through their life and purpose and their contribution and value to 'the world'. There is an attraction in the inner strength this spiritually provides. Often-quoted businesspeople, such as author Stephen Covey and Body Shop founder Anita Roddick, display spiritual intelligence through a clear set of personal values and beliefs which drive their actions.

Psychologically there is also attraction in working for an organization that is clear about the guiding principles of how people in the organization should behave towards each other and how they can expect to be treated by the organization. This is especially so when the organization's values align with employees' own. If they don't, there is a mismatch.

I was recently involved in a training course for an organization whose espoused values were fresh thinking, fun and freedom to act. The course aimed to help people to better understand what this meant in their role as managers. One of the delegates actively disengaged herself from the proceedings. She said that the way the programme was being run re-inforced to her that she did not share the values that underpinned the development programme. She therefore found it difficult to whole-heartedly embrace the organization's ethos. For her the event merely confirmed that she was not in an organization where she wanted to stay.

Values underpin the way an organization does business

One the dangers of a values approach is that the values are just words and are therefore tokenistic.

I have seen organizational values work in favour of employee engagement when they are embedded in the organization and all other systems, processes and behaviours are aligned to them. An example of this is the people management process. As Figure 5.2 shows, the development of a competency framework for an organization becomes stronger when it is aligned to the organization's vision and values. A competency framework in turn can help decide how people are recruited and on the selection processes used. For example, assessment centres can be established to assess candidates' knowledge, skills and behaviours against competencies. A performance review system can be developed that reviews not only what each individual has achieved but how well they perform against competencies, etc.

RECRUITMENT AND SELECTION	PERFORMANCE MANAGEMENT AND COACHING	SUCCESSION PLANNING AND TALENT MANAGEMENT	TRAINING AND DEVELOPMENT	REWARD AND RECOGNITION
COMPETENCIES				
VALUES				
VISION				

Figure 5.2 Vision, values and people management

Case studies

What can be learned in terms of employee engagement from those organizations that do have a strong set of values? Here are some examples.

Vodafone

Arin Sarun, CEO of Vodafone, is a strong believer in the power of organizational values. He explains:

> Our statement of values defines our culture. It reflects our four passions – customers, employees, results, the world around us. These passions are the guide-post for our 60,000 employees worldwide. We use them to identify the people we want. We look for team players, we look for people who are customer focused, we look for people who embody our brand and we look for people who will go the extra mile to enhance our reputation.

Strong brands have well-defined values. Vodafone uses these to ensure that it attracts and retains team members who will embody the brand.

John Lewis

Ever since 1918, when its first profit-sharing scheme was introduced, retailer John Lewis has had a clear mission. The first principle in the John Lewis Partnership constitution states that the organization's ultimate purpose is 'the happiness of all its members, through their worthwhile and satisfying employment in a successful business'.

Former Chairman Sir Stuart Hampson explained in an article in *Director* in 2007: 'In retailing, some jobs can be very routine and hard. Our ownership structure, which allows our partners (employees) to share the responsibilities of ownership as well as its rewards – profit, knowledge and power – helps create job satisfaction and engagement.

Yet it is clear that co-ownership is just the starting point. The power kicks in when combined with the full engagement of employees in 'co-creation' of value. Another of John Lewis's principles is to aim to make 'sufficient profit... to sustain its commercial vitality, to finance its continued development, to distribute a share of those profits to members...' This determines the partnership's management style, says Sir Stuart. 'People who are very commercial but have no sense of staff engagement are not judged to be successful managers here, and our reward, development and promotion strategies are geared towards these twin attributes.'

The partnership employs some 'hugely talented and commercial people' who have sacrificed the opportunity to earn more elsewhere – 'We don't have share options, for example' – for what they see as the greater satisfaction of creating happy teams and satisfied customers.

In consultation with its partners, John Lewis recently developed six elements of behaviour that it believes define the way it deals with all its stakeholders, including partners, customers and suppliers. These are honesty, respect, recognition of others, working together, showing enterprise and – as a result – achieving more. At the time of writing the group had just announced one of its most successful years to date.

John Lewis is an example of an organization that has a mission that determines the organization's way of working and its management style. Its strong core beliefs instil a sense of pride and success in its employees.

Microsoft

Microsoft is another organization that has a strong set of values that helps it attract like-minded people. Steve Bulmer, its CEO, explains:

At Microsoft, we look for people who share a set of values. We believe in, and talk to our people about, integrity, passion for technology, passion for customers. We look for people who are open and respectful and dedicated to making others better. Software development is a collaborative exercise. We look for people who are dedicated to self-improvement, who every day ask: 'How can I be better? What did I do wrong? How do I improve?' We want our people to set big, bold goals while having a great sense of accountability. That is fundamental in our culture.

We look for people who are incredibly bright and hard-working. In any job in the company, I want to have someone who is brighter and harder working than the guy who is doing their job at our competitors.

Key learning points

▌ Organizational values serve as a strong template for the recruitment of like-minded people to your business.

▌ When the values that are espoused and behaviours that employees see in an organization are fully aligned this creates a strong organizational culture and can give meaning to people's work.

A PROCESS FOR DEFINING ORGANIZATIONAL VALUES

One of the recommendations I made to the optician retailer we worked with to help increase the levels of employee engagement was to develop a set of organizational values. These, I suggested, could be a set of guiding principles for the business going forward. I also suggested that once the values were embedded they could also help strengthen their brand and contribute towards the organization becoming an employer of choice.

In practice, values are best defined by employees in the business itself rather than just the senior leadership team. When senior executives define the values alone there can be a problem because what senior executives want to be important in the business can be very different from day-to-day reality. As an example, one CEO I know of a large corporation defined the businesses values with the board. One of the values they set was 'trust'. In fact if they had asked employees they would have seen that this was very far from what seemed to be important in the day-to-day running of the business. Every working day employees at each office were photographed going in and out of the building. The CEO was not aware of this as when he visited different sites the facilities managers were instructed to hide the cameras in the reception area. Understandably employees were suspicious of the values and felt they were an example of 'do as I say, not as I do'.

To make sure that values are truly embraced, we normally run a series of short workshops and focus groups to begin the process. During the sessions we ask groups of employees, drawn from across the organization, what they consider is and should be important as guiding principles for the organization. We collect the output and together with a sponsor and project team pull together what appear to be the key values of the organization. These can number up to six. In practice, we find that any more than this number and the values become forgotten.

When developing a set of values, however, it is important to recognize that certain values will be 'lived' at present in the organization; others may be desired values – ie those the organization wishes to embody but which it may not be yet epitomizing. This is fine if work is being done to lessen the dissonance with the value, but not if there is never going to be an improvement in this area.

For example, we worked with one government department that developed a value to be 'human'. It knew from customer research that often this is not how employees were perceived in the eyes of the public, although the department wanted to be perceived this way. Therefore the department knew it had to work hard to demonstrate the human side of its nature in all its transactions with customers.

Another organization with whom we worked had a vision of 'inspiring customers'. Its values were customer service, teamwork, integrity and learning. It developed a competency framework that embedded these four values into the desired skills and behaviours for all levels of employees. The values and competencies in turn drove the recruitment and selection process. They were the criteria against which people were performance managed, and according to which promotion decisions were made and development offered. The values were also brought to life through a recognition scheme that gave credit to people who had delivered inspirational service. What was successful here was that as the values had been developed by employees there was little resistance to them.

Key learning points

▌ Actively involve employees in the development of values to ensure that they are more likely to be accepted as the basis for 'how we do things around here'.

▌ Recognize that there may be a difference between the organization's actual values and those desired by the organization. Take steps to bridge this gap.

TRANSLATING VALUES INTO BEHAVIOURS

Often values are published in organizations, pasted on the walls and that is expected to change the culture. Successful organizations bring values to life in everything that happens in the organization.

In order for that to transpire, employees need to know how to translate the values – what do the values actually mean people have to do in their everyday working lives? If people understand the meaning, how it links to what they do, what it looks like, what positive impact it can have on them and their colleagues, then they will be more motivated to put the values into practice.

Each value needs to be made explicit by describing the behaviours that epitomize it. In order to do this, it is best, again, to involve as many people throughout the organization as possible to generate the behaviours.

Having held a series of workshops with a cross-section of employees from the optician retailer to define brand values, we then worked with a group of 16 people to develop the behaviours that sat under each value. The group participants represented all levels and functions of employees both at head office and throughout the store network. For each value they generated ideas about what they individually believed they would do or say to bring the value to life.

Next, each set of behaviours was prioritized by the group to arrive at between four and six behaviours that described each value and which were applicable to everyone. Each person from the group then took responsibility for gaining feedback from their peer groups about the relevance of the values. Following this feedback the values were introduced via a one-day conference for all employees. This brought the values to life in an interactive and participative fashion. The values were then reinforced by incorporating them into the performance management system.

Here is an example of how values have been translated into behaviours in one organization so that employees know what is expected of themselves and others. The behaviours guidelines act as a statement of the type of person the organization expects employees to be and what they believe in. So for the value 'enabling' the underpinning behaviours are:

- involving others in decision making, encouraging alternative opinions;
- enabling freedom of action through providing clarity on direction, boundaries and scope;
- sharing useful information and experience, helping others to make informed decisions;
- developing others' performance through providing a mixture of supportive and challenging feedback;
- encouraging others to show personal initiative, taking responsibility, and learning from their mistakes.

For 'innovation' the underpinning behaviours are:

▎ finding new and different ways of doing things

▎ continually reviewing and improving existing processes;

▎ challenging the status quo.

Here is an example of one organization that has used the development of values to good effect in the implementation of an employee engagement programme.

Airtours case study

At the same time as facing increasing competition and aggressive price wars, the UK-based package tour company Airtours found that low levels of employee engagement and high staff turnover were leading in turn to low levels of customer satisfaction. The company decided that it needed to produce a strategy to help distinguish the Airtours brand in the marketplace, develop higher levels of customer satisfaction and retention and increase levels of employee engagement.

The board decided to create an internal brand values programme to support an external brand repositioning campaign. After rigorous debate, the leadership team agreed not only to define the brand values for the organization but also to commit to defining and role modelling the desired behaviours.

At a two-day off-site event the 25 members of the senior management team defined the values that they believed truly epitomized the Airtours brand. These were to be:

▌ creative and inspiring;

▌ genuine and trustworthy;

▌ friendly and enthusiastic;

▌ organized and professional.

For each value they defined five behavioural indicators demonstrating at every level of the business how the value could be translated into tangible behaviour.

Employees' initial reaction to the brand values programme was one of some cynicism, with many employees viewing the campaign as 'flavour of the month'. However, the managing director made a public commitment about his own personal behaviour change and changes he expected from others. There then followed a teaser campaign to preview the values. A values director was appointed at a senior level to develop the programme, reporting to a joint committee of senior managers headed by the managing director. All employees were invited to a half-day workshop that would introduce them to the values and behaviours in more depth. During these workshops employees were encouraged by trained internal facilitators to debate what the values meant in their particular work area. Ongoing values forums and training linked to the values were also put in place to reinforce the message. In addition 'value days' events took place on a monthly basis to focus on an individual value. These were delivered in a fun and interactive manner via competitions and team events.

To embed the values further the performance management system was changed to incorporate the values and a 360-degree feedback process based on the values was introduced. The values are now part of the pay and reward system. In addition, a review of processes took place to bring them in line with the values.

The company measured changes in customer and employee perception of the brand as the values programme progressed. Over the course of three years customers' ratings of their overall holiday experience moved from 67 per cent very satisfied to 80 per cent, and customer loyalty and intention to repurchase from 70 per cent to 78 per cent. In staff surveys 91 per cent of staff supported the values and 75 per cent believed that they helped them to identify ways for the organization to improve.

Key learning points

▍ Defining the behaviours that epitomize each value is a powerful way of bringing the values to life.

▍ To become part of the culture of an organization, values need to be well communicated.

▍ Linking the values to the organization's performance management system is a powerful way of reinforcing them.

A REMINDER

The fact that an organization takes steps to develop an employer brand, actively develops its organizational values and takes steps to promote CSR does not in turn guarantee that employees will be engaged with the organization and go the extra mile. As outlined earlier, it is important make sure that your engagement strategy is holistic and addresses the key drivers that will ensure that employees truly are engaged with the organization. It is all very well to increase the levels of applicants that you receive for positions in your organization but once employed the way that employees are treated needs to match the expectations that are set.

INCREASED WORKLOAD AND STRESS LEVELS

Research indicates that engagement is more likely than not to be associated with a good work–life balance as well as putting in place policies that are likely to promote employee welfare. Why is this? According to an ISR annual study of 400,000 employees in the United States, stress at work is increasing. In 2006, 31 per cent of those surveyed said they found it difficult to balance work and personal responsibilities, compared to 25 per cent in 2005. Regarding workload, 43 per cent think their workload is excessive, up from 39 per cent in 2005, and 46 per cent (an increase of 5 per cent) are bothered by excessive pressure on the job. Stress, workload and work–life balance are becoming increasingly hot topics.

External pressures from competition and technology that promotes the fast paced 24/7 global economy have begun blurring the boundaries between work and home life. The fact that BlackBerry® and other mobile technology allow us to log on to the internet at any time of the day and night and in any place across the globe means that theoretically we may never need to pause from working and are constantly contactable.

A 2004 study found that 27 per cent workers were overwhelmed by how much work they had to do and 29 per cent often or very often did not have the time to process or reflect on the work that they did. Overwork often leads to stress and physical and psychological health problems. It is clear that stressed employees are less likely to be engaged and productive in the workplace.

Yet certainly many organizations fail to recognize the impact of overwork. I know of several organizations that have told their managers that they need to double their output in the next three years with the same resources. These organizations emphasize the need to work smarter but have not given managers the tools or training to do this. Approximately half of all disengaged employees say that their work has a negative impact on their health and well-being.

This phenomenon is not confined to the Western world of work. Indian call centre environments are experiencing many of the issues encountered by European centres. With the growth of outsourcing to the Indian subcontinent call centre managers have the increasing dilemma of motivating employees in an environment that is highly controlled and where performance is tightly monitored and measured against targets. At the same time employees are encouraged to take responsibility for both their team and their own performance. The pay system encourages employees to perform better by giving rewards to higher performers.

Studies show that the erratic shift patterns are a problem for people who are married or have families. Working at night is not acceptable socially for many Indian women. After working on night shifts with impatient or angry customers for a few weeks, employees report feeling unwell and stressed. Almost one in two workers admit to smoking too much to alleviate the pressure. In a recent study 88.6 per cent of those workers surveyed disagreed that their jobs were an enriching experience. Turnover in some call centres runs to 100–200 per cent in a year. The reasons attributed to high labour turnover are the pressures of the job, lack of promotion opportunities, working time, work–life balance, 'phone rage' and the repetitive nature of the work.

In the United Kingdom the Health and Safety Executive (HSE) has devised stress management standards to help employers assess the issues that may cause stress in the workplace and to take active steps to address these. The HSE has identified six primary sources of stress at work:

▌ demands: workload, work patterns and the work environment;

▌ control: how much say individuals have in the way that they do their work;

▌ support: encouragement, sponsorship and resources provided by managers and colleagues;

▌ relationships: whether positive working is promoted to avoid conflict;

▌ role: the degree to which people understand their role in the organization;

▌ change: how organizational change is managed and communicated.

The agency explains that stress is an often misused term for a range of health problems that may lead to long-term mental and physical ill health. Its studies show that people with chronic physical disorders such as back pain and those experiencing financial or domestic difficulties are more likely to experience depression.

As the level of stress tolerance varies between individuals, it suggests using an online health profiling tool such as the Wellness Index to help individuals assess and take action to reduce their levels of stress. This looks at individuals holistically and their:

- satisfaction with lifestyle;
- ability to cope with pressure;
- attitude towards wellness and health;
- management of personal health and well-being issues;
- active lifestyle;
- levels of physical activity;
- mental well-being;
- pace of life;
- physical health;
- stress levels.

Individuals receive a confidential report advising them how to improve their general well-being.

The employer receives an overview of the state of well-being of workers in the organization as a whole, allowing the employer to identify parts of the organization that may be more susceptible to stress. The overview provides the employer with recommended interventions to help reduce the causes of stress.

Case studies

First Direct

Financial services organization First Direct consciously created a mission of a 'great place to work' and carefully thought about the needs of its employees. Since 80 per cent of then are women often working in a 24-hour environment, it paid extra attention to their needs for personal security, for example with controlled parking spaces. It also offered a large crèche facility. To give employees and customers the best possible experience, new employees are given a thorough five-week induction, accredited training and rewards for successful performance. Managers carry out a twice-yearly engagement survey among employees – and act on the results.

First Direct has a well-thought-out retention strategy, including resource deployment so the employee isn't overstretched and can deliver to the customer.

> ### Google
>
> At Google Inc, product and service developments such as Google News, Froogle (an online product and price comparison service) and Gmail have all been the result of employees' ideas. The culture that has developed at Google is one of 'Twenty Percent Time'. To give employees control at work, engineers are expected to spend one fifth of their working time putting energy into projects that interest them personally. If an idea has merit it is incubated and developed further by the company. Over half the organization's product launches have been created as a result of this scheme. 'Twenty Percent Time' also acts as a powerful recruitment attraction for new employees.

Key learning point

However you assess as an organization the stress levels in your organization, a key learning point is to take action proactively to reduce the causes of stress in your business.

WORK–LIFE BALANCE

The same issues of work–life balance affected the team members of the optician retailer I worked with. Interestingly, their survey results scored very poorly for the company being family focused or promoting flexible working. The HR director met resistance from the senior management team when she proposed introducing flexible working patterns. The HR director herself had young children and only worked four days a week. Yet she was the only woman on the senior management team, many of whom had partners who did not work. The challenge was to demonstrate the benefits of flexible working patterns to the executive group.

Interestingly enough, many best practice examples can be found among government departments in the United Kingdom. Departments such as the Treasury and Department of Media, Culture and Sport have family-friendly policies that include:

▐ Flexible working. Employees have to be present for the core hours of 10.00 am to 3.00 pm. Other than this they have flexibility in when they work and what hours they put in to make up their 38 hours a week.

▌ Crèche and child care facilities.

▌ Vouchers.

▌ Family days when parents are encouraged to bring their children to work.

▌ Fun days and outings for families.

Work–life balance and quality of life is already an important topic for workers and set to become more important, so senior leaders need to recognize that taking action to address this need really matters.

THE LONG-HOURS CULTURE

There still exists in many organizations the sense that to achieve and progress in the business, you have to put in more than your contractual hours of work. One of my clients is a large corporation that has recently built a new office housing 4,000 of its head office staff. The design of the building includes a street where there are shops, banks, hairdressers, dry cleaners and restaurants so that employees who work flexibly can use the facilities whenever they wish. Unfortunately, the facilities are barely used outside the lunchtime period. Although employees know that they can work flexibly, the reality is that managers expect their staff to work from the traditional 9.00 am to 5.00 pm. The thought of coming in early and leaving a 3.00 pm to have one's hair done or to go shopping in the street is tacitly discouraged. There needs to be a paradigm shift in the way managers view work in most organizations to make a positive work–life balance a reality.

What best practice organizations have in common is that the work–life balance is taken seriously and the long-hours culture is discouraged. With work-related stress increasing, companies are introducing more flexible working.

A positive work–life balance delivers staff loyalty, employee motivation, reduced absenteeism, the recruitment and retention of a talented work-force and improved customer service. As Sarah Jackson, Chief Executive of Working Families, a work–life balance campaigning organization, says:

> There are basic, bottom-line financial advantages in getting flexible working and a work–life balance culture embedded in your organization. My 'big picture' business benefit is that if you engage your employees so that they feel they're supported and valued, they will give so much more and that will be translated into business success.

Leading employers know that it's not just about women and babies but all their employees, across a lifetime of work. And employers are beginning to understand that there is more to it than simply looking at recruitment and retention issues. They are thinking about what the business needs and how they can deliver that with the people they've got.

Best Buy case study

One company that has completely revolutionized the world of work is Minneapolis company Best Buy. Best Buy is a US consumer electronics company. It operates over 940 stores in the United States and Canada and has 90,000 employees working in retail outlets and its head office. It sells electronic equipment and mobile and internet equipment as well as offering installation and maintenance services.

Best Buy has developed a company culture based on ROWE (results-only work environment). This puts the focus on results and employees can work when and as long as they want as long as the job gets done. Attendance at meetings is optional.

The concept began five years ago when a pilot study with 300 people began to introduce flexible working methods. One of the downsides that the pilot study identified was that 'flexible' was only flexible from the employer's point of view. Employees were still expected to be present during the core hours of 10.00 am and 4.00 pm. They only had discretion on when they worked between 8.00 am and 10.00 am and 4.00 pm and 6.00 pm.

The company's ROWE scheme is a complete shift in paradigm. It puts the emphasis on performance and outputs rather than the length of time that the employee is present. The company has adopted this approach in its Minneapolis headquarters, which employs over 4,000 people. After a pilot period, over 60 per cent have transitioned to ROWE. Each manager agrees with his or her team member what the desired output for each position and work plan will be, as well as how performance will be measured.

Best Buy is reporting increased engagement levels as a result of the scheme, including lower levels of stress. It also has had a positive impact for the company on recruitment, as both internal and external job candidates are rating work–life balance as important as monetary compensation. On the downside, the company recognizes that this is a difficult paradigm shift for some managers to make. Typical initial reactions are that the scheme is not practical or that people will take advantage of it. In practice this has not happened, although the organization recognizes that people need to find new ways of communicating to make ROWE work. At first the amount of e-mail that people who were on the scheme sent was overwhelming as they felt the need to prove that they were working. The organization is also conscious of the risk that longer-term employees may feel less attached to the company. However, to date the scheme has proved effective. The organization is considering extending the programme to its retail stores and has had much interest from other companies about what can be learned.

Key learning points

▌ It is possible to rethink the way we work in organizations today.

▌ Piloting new ways of working can be a gradual way of changing the paradigm about work.

▌ Innovative organizations focus more on employees' outputs rather than when or where they achieved these.

DIFFERENT TYPES OF FLEXIBLE WORKING

Best practice organizations adopt a variety of different approaches to flexible working. There are different types of flexible work arrangements that employers can offer their team members. These include:

▌ staggered hours where staff members start and finish their days at different times;

▌ job-sharing where several people work together to cover a full-time post;

▌ compressed hours where an employee works normal hours over a longer day;

▌ annualized hours where the employee works a total number of hours over a year rather than per week;

▌ term-time working where employees take unpaid leave;

▌ homeworking where employees work from home either full time or part time.

▌ flexi-time where staff members have a flexible start and finish time based around core hours;

▌ sabbaticals where employees are given a paid or unpaid break from work for an agreed period;

▌ schemes where members of staff are given time off (paid or unpaid) to work on a voluntary basis, for example for Voluntary Service Overseas.

EMPLOYEE WELFARE

Along with flexible working, best practice organizations focus on developing strategies for employee welfare. These strategies can encompass a range of benefits and there is a growing trend to make them as wide ranging as possible so that the employee has a choice.

However, only one quarter of organizations have an employee well-being strategy or similar initiative in place, according to the Chartered Institute of Personnel and Development's latest absence research. The *Absence Management Survey 2006*, which questioned more than 1,000 employers from the private, public and voluntary sectors, also revealed that 42 per cent of public sector organizations had such a strategy, compared with only 22 per cent of private sector firms. Private health insurance was found to be the most common investment in well-being, with 60 per cent providing it to some employees.

Henry Stewart, founder and Chief Executive of Happy, the training company, which came in number 11 the *Financial Times* list of best UK workplaces in 2007, believes that focusing on making stakeholders happy increases profits. 'Happiness is a means to an end', he says. The company, which has 46 staff, offers a range of flexible working options, and actively helps employees work out the best solution for them, rather than waiting for employees to approach their managers. 'People work best when they feel good about themselves, so the role of management here is to help people feel good', says Stewart.

So what sort of policies are needed? There are basic welfare strategies that all organizations should have in place such as policies that promote diversity and equality. Many organizations now offer health facilities and have developed family-friendly policies. The move is towards a cafeteria suite of options that allow employees to pick and chose.

The range of welfare options offered will very much depend on the marketplace and the demographics of the workforce. In China, for example, the PRC government is aggressively developing new laws and regulations to improve the welfare of employees. These include regulations to increase social security contributions. Many provinces also have clarified tax provisions related to pension rules.

Case studies

Genetech

Genetech, the US biotechnology company which came top in the Fortune 100 Best Companies to Work for 2006, offers its employees flexible scheduling. At Genetech 49 per cent of the workforce is female and flexible scheduling is seen as a most critical benefit for working mothers. People can work the hours to suit them, there are no core hours. The organization's child-friendly policy includes child care options and time off for new parents.

Dupont

Pharmaceutical company Dupont, based in Delaware, has a core value of sustaining a respectful work environment. Every employee attends a CREW (Creating a Respectful Environment at Work) programme. It has a zero-tolerance policy towards sexual harassment, workplace harassment and intimidation. It provides the same benefits plan for all employees, including in-vitro fertilization benefits, long-term care insurance and paid adoption leave.

Ritz Carlton

The Ritz Carlton Hotel Palm Beach was closed in 2006 for a six-month renovation period. Ritz Carlton had never closed a hotel for refurbishment before and was keen to retain its employees for the six-month period of closure. To do this it provided its employees with several options. The first was called 'task forcing' where managers and staff were offered the opportunity of job postings in different Ritz Carlton and Marriott Hotels all over the United States. Around 140 people took up the opportunity to work temporarily elsewhere. Ritz Carlton took up the cost of flights, accommodation, etc. One of the benefits of this on their return is that they were able to share best practice.

A similar number of staff decided to take five months off, with the company continuing to pay the employer portion of benefits. This allowed them to stay at home with their children, travel or study for the five-month period. Finally, around 150 employees took part in a community volunteer programme where they could get their wages and benefits for up to 40 hours per week working for the local community. As a result of the fair treatment they were given in the closure period, 85 per cent of employees returned to the hotel when it reopened.

Business Development Bank of Canada

The Business Development Bank of Canada employs 1,700 people. It has increased its engagement score by developing a range of flexible benefits to offer its employees. The new package was extensively communicated to employees. It contains a variety of different options including:

- buying and selling up to five days of holiday entitlement;

- receiving cash instead of benefits;

- flexible healthcare benefits;

- an employee savings plan where the company matches the amount saved;

- pension contributions.

Employees can switch between benefits whenever they want. The programme is communicated via a comprehensive website. The company has found that potential recruits as well as current employees pay attention to the flexible benefit scheme.

Great Little Box Company

The Great Little Box Company is a US manufacturing business that has won many accolades for being a great company to work for. The business is keen to encourage the well-being of its employees. It has newly built premises that include a gym, a sandpit for beach volleyball and a basketball court. Being on the waterfront it also has kayak and canoeing facilities. It also has an active hiking club. The company gives points to employees for doing exercise which they can use for prizes. Free fruit is offered to all employees as a matter of course. At Christmas the CEO asks employees what their children would like for a gift. He makes it his business to see that they receive this. The results of these initiatives is a tight culture and a focus on customer service.

3M

At 3M, the manufacturer with products ranging from adhesives to floppy disks, staff are encouraged to take regular sabbaticals where they can do something innovative. If they come back with an idea that then turns into a product, they can share in its success. This benefit helps to reinforce 3M's value of innovation.

Key learning points

▌ The welfare policy of each organization needs to be designed with the needs of different demographic groups in mind.

▌ Giving employees flexibility and choice in the welfare benefits that they receive is important.

▌ Welfare benefits should have a cultural fit with the organization.

JOB DESIGN AND RESOURCES

A further aspect of employee welfare that is often overlooked but which studies show is of great importance is job design. Part of employee's well-being is feeling that they have appropriately stimulating and challenging work to do. In addition, they need to feel that they have adequate resources to do the job well.

The area of the business that scored the lowest in the optician retailer's engagement survey was the post room. In delving deeper into why this was we discovered that the majority of the work (putting information in envelopes for branches) was seen as repetitive and boring. The department had been promised automated facilities some time ago but these had not materialized. This added to the feeling that the work was laborious, repetitive and slow.

The design of jobs themselves is important to the level of engagement and ultimately has an impact on health. In the United Kingdom the Office for National Statistics data show routine workers are 2.8 times more likely to die by the age of 64 than high-level managers. Experts report high-level workers as least likely to die in accidents, violent attacks and from suicide. Professor Danny Dorling, an expert in health inequalities at Sheffield University, said on the BBC website: 'Those in better paid, more prestigious jobs are less likely to suffer violence, behave differently, are treated better and value their work more.'

FEELING VALUED

The engagement levels of the post room employees were not helped by the fact that their manager was based in another building. They saw little of him and the manager certainly did not demonstrate that he cared.

Fundamental to the overall feeling of well-being that an employee has is that their direct line manager cares about them as a person.

I was asked recently to work with one team in a technical environment to help improve their engagement scores. When I sat down with the manager who had been managing the team for two years, he could tell me very little about them as people other than their job functions and how long they had been with the department. Little wonder engagement scores were low. It certainly came across to me that the manager cared little about his team members and was not concerned for their welfare. When we started doing work with the team as a whole, a raft of interesting facts emerged about them as people: one had eight children, another was a trained counsellor, yet another was a railway enthusiast, a further one a Scout leader and another a divorcee with three young children and a sick mother-in-law who was dependent on the employee. To his subsequent shame the manager had taken no interest in any of the team's well-being or the time to find out what made them tick as people.

My consultancy is often asked to facilitate team-building events and activities. One of the most powerful means we find of creating stronger ties in a team is for the manager and team members to find out more about each other as people. Showing an interest in others' emotional and physical well-being is fundamental to employee engagement.

Checklist

What is your organization doing in terms of CSR, employer brand, organizational values, the welfare of staff?

What can your organization do to increase the activities it undertakes in the area of CSR?

What can you do to strengthen your employer brand?

What are your organizational values?

How aligned are these to organizational behaviours, and if they are not, what can you do about it?

How can your organization improve the work–life balance it offers its employees?

What additions can you make to the welfare package of your staff that would increase levels of engagement?

This chapter has investigated how employee well-being impacts levels of engagement. It has outlined the importance of employee welfare as well as the steps many organizations are taking to create a strong employer brand to attract and retain talent. The chapter also focused on the importance of flexible working and different types of employee welfare policies including work–life balance. The next chapter focuses on the importance of information.

6

Information

The second letter of WIFI stands for information. Having a clear vision of where the organization is going and what it wants to achieve and communicating this effectively is an essential element in binding employees together. Having clarity around organizational goals is essential in helping employees to know where they are going and why and how they fit into achieving those goals. The regularity and appropriateness of information at all levels is a key driver of engagement.

This chapter looks at the cascade process of information giving throughout a business. Simple as it sounds, the process of giving information is something that many organizations fail to get right. This chapter provides examples of different best practices as well as looking at the pivotal role of senior managers in this process.

WHERE ARE WE GOING?

Typical problems faced by employees are that there is either too much information or a scarcity of it. In the case of the optician retailer, following the merger of the two businesses employees were floundering: they did not know the future direction of the company. There were widespread rumours about further redundancies and closures. It was clear that the senior leaders in the business needed quickly to create and depict a compelling vision for the future in order to stave off further unrest.

COMMUNICATING A CLEAR SENSE OF DIRECTION

Senior managers set the tone for engagement in any organization. In particular what they say and do is critical in driving higher levels of employee engagement. This is particularly relevant when it comes to the second building block of WIFI: information.

Research and consultancy firm ISR found that 73 per cent of employees in best practice organizations believed that the management of their organization provided a clear sense of direction, compared with 46 per cent of ordinary companies. The same study found that best practice organizations were more likely to focus on long-term goals and creating stakeholder value rather than shareholder value. The reason for this appears to be that employees want to be associated with a sense of purpose, to know what the organization stands for and where it is going.

Communicating a clear vision of the future is one of the most important factors that senior managers can influence. This is the most important task for new leaders in their first 100 days, over and above spending time learning about the business and developing a relationship with the executive team. It is also something that leaders who have been in the job for some time need to reinforce constantly. 'People should see the clear link between what they do and the longer-term results' says Earl Sasser, Baker Foundation Professor at Harvard Business School. So, when researchers look at successful organizations where employees are committed and engaged, there are several things those organizations have in common: a compelling vision of the future and a clearly communicated strategy.

BEING CLEAR ON TERMINOLOGY

During discussions with the board of the optician retailer about the need for a clear vision for the organization, it became clear that there was some confusion around the terminology I was using. There are a number of terms that get banded around in relation to organizational vision, mission, strategy and values. Often organizations say they have a vision, when in fact this is a mission. To help clarify terminology, here is a definition of the different words used:

▌ vision: a picture of a desired future state that is sufficiently appealing and compelling to drive change forward; the 'where we want to be';

▌ mission: the purpose of the organization; the 'what we want to achieve';

▌ values: the underlying principles and ethics that drive the organization; the 'how we want to act to guide us towards our vision';

▌ goals: the objectives or targets that the organization is trying to achieve; the 'what we need to achieve our mission';

▌ strategy: the approach that the organization is adopting to achieve the goals; the 'how we will achieve our goals';

▌ behaviours: the way in which people in the organization act in terms of what they do and say that brings the strategy and desired culture to life; the 'what we will say and do to bring our values to life'.

Figure 6.1 explains the interrelationships. Vision sits at the top of the drawing; this is where the organization is driving. The mission supports the vision. On the left of the diagram is the 'what': what needs to be achieved, the organizational goals and the strategy that the business will adopt to achieve these. On the right-hand side of the drawing is the 'how': the organizational values that act as guiding principles for the business

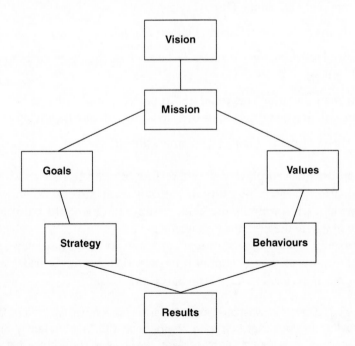

Figure 6.1 The where, the what and the how

and the behaviours that are aligned to them. The combination of the 'what' and the 'how' leads to business results and organizational success.

DEVELOPING A VISION OF THE FUTURE

A strong vision provides a powerful image of a compelling future state. This can engage and inspire employees so that they know the journey that they are taking. Mike Newnham, vice president of business solutions at telecommunications company Orange, explains: 'Communicating your vision is critical, whether you are leading a small entrepreneurial company or a large corporate.'

A vision sets the direction for the organization, where the business wants to be. Having a vision for your organization means you stretch the organization beyond its current grasp. The criteria for a good vision are that it is memorable, meaningful and inspirational. Here are some examples of organizational visions. They may not be meaningful to you because you are not employed by the organization. However, which do you find memorable and inspirational?

▌ healthcare organization: 'Taking care of the life in our hands';

▌ up-market hotel chain: 'Discovery';

▌ entertainment group: 'Dream, Believe, Dare, Do';

▌ financial services organization: 'To be the first choice for customers and colleagues';

▌ card manufacturer and retailer: 'To enrich people's lives, help them express their feelings, celebrate occasions and enhance their relationships';

▌ logistics company: 'People, Customers, Profits'.

A vision provides employees with a picture of a future state to which the organization is striving. Organizations with successful employee engagement programmes use their vision statements to paint a clear picture of where the organization wants to be.

For example, telecommunications company Vodafone have developed a vision: 'To enrich our customers' lives and to be the worlds' mobile communications leader'. CEO Arin Sarun explains:

> Our vision identifies what businesses we are in and why we are in them. We provide services that help people connect with friends, family and colleagues, and connect with information. We can stand up and say that we enrich our customers' lives; that is the privilege of the business we are in.

We are very clear about who we are – a mobile wireless communications company. We do not have any landlines or fixed lines and we do not intend to have them. We are very clear about what we want to be – the world leader. We do not want to be second. We want to be first.

Midlands Co-operative case study

Midlands Co-operative Society created a powerful vision to drive change. Midlands Co-operative Society, or Midlands Co-op as it is better known, is the second largest independent retail cooperative society in the United Kingdom. It employs over 7,000 staff and has gross sales in excess of £744 million. It also has a substantial investment property portfolio. Its principal activities are food and non-food retail, travel retail, funeral services and transport. It has 375 trading outlets, ranging from superstores and convenience stores to funeral homes and post offices based in the Midlands.

Midlands Co-op developed in its current form following several mergers of cooperative societies. However, it was evident by the early 2000s that Midlands Co-op was suffering from lack of economies of scale. This, together with poor sales performance in the light of increasing competition in the retail sector and a lack of reduction in cost base led the Midlands Co-op to recognize the need for major change. In 2003 the chief executive and the senior management team undertook a full strategic review of the way forward for the organization. Subsequently, it was decided that a change programme should be created to create a new culture across the business. Central to this was the need to engage both employees and customers as it was believed that this would be the key to the Co-op's long-term success.

The Co-op recognized that it needed to change the way things were done in the organization to make it more competitive. This, senior managers realized, meant changing the culture of the organization. The first step was to define the current way of doing things throughout the Co-op. Recognizing that culture is the glue that binds an organization together and can be invisible to people in an organization, the senior management team invited my consultancy team to conduct a series of employee and customer focus groups to help the Co-op better understand its current position.

The findings of the research indicated that in terms of customer engagement the Co-op had many loyal customers who had traditionally shopped with the company for a long time. The key strengths of the Co-op from a customer perspective were the location and convenience of their stores. However, particularly in food retail, the Co-op could not compete on price or range with the larger food outlets.

Some of the cultural indicators that we discovered when conducting the internal employee focus groups included a highly 'siloed' organization where managers were still referred to as 'Mr' and where there was a divide between head office and front-line staff. The culture was perceived as hier-archical and risk averse. In particular, although many employees had worked for the organization for 20 years or more, there was a strong feeling of lack of recognition of effort and achievement. This was cited as a major area of concern by 75 per cent of employees taking part in the focus groups.

We presented the outcomes from the research to the CEO and senior leadership team. They recommended that the starting point for change was the development of an organizational vision and a set of supporting values. The organizational vision and values would then drive the resulting mission and strategy for the Co-op. The vision that was developed was 'Making a difference'. A set of supporting values that underpin the way the Co-op does its business were developed in a collaborative manner with a cross-section of employees.

The senior management team recognized that that the communication of the vision and values would be key to embedding them in the organ-ization. In 2004 the senior management team appointed a general manager for culture and service, thus highlighting the importance that the Co-op gave to the culture change programme. She explains:

Once the vision and values were communicated we were able to develop a strategy to help deliver our vision and embed our values. This strategy, set out as a road map, concentrated first on employee satisfaction and engagement and then improvements to the service we deliver to our external customers. Key to its successful implementation was the robust communication plan that accompanied the programme.

Key learning points

▌ Creating a powerful and compelling vision for the future can help drive employee engagement.

▌ Key to the successful buy-in for the vision is how it is then communi-cated to employees.

CREATING A COMPELLING ORGANIZATIONAL VISION

If your organization currently has an organizational vision, is it still appropriate in current trading conditions? Is the vision motivational as well as inspirational? Rather than leaving the vision to be solely created by the senior team, my recommendation is that all levels of the organization have an opportunity to contribute to this and to see how it can come to life in their working environment.

The optician retailer had an organizational vision but this was poorly communicated and understood. It had also become tired and uninspiring. To reinvigorate the vision, we ran a series of meetings to generate ideas at all levels of the organization. This was important as it gained buy-in from employees at an early point. The sessions focused on what sort of organization customers, employees and other stakeholders wanted to create for the future. We recorded the outputs and together with the executive board created a short, inspirational and memorable phrase that captured the essence of the responses.

A short period of testing then followed to ensure that the vision was relevant to all those involved. In the spirit of employee engagement we encouraged feedback on the proposed vision to check that it was motivational.

The next stage was to communicate the vision to all of the organization in an interactive manner. I recommended that the business communicated their vision and values together so that they became more meaningful and employees could see the bigger picture.

COMMUNICATING THE VISION IN AN ENGAGING MANNER

Steve Bulmer, CEO of Microsoft says that all leaders have to ask:

> What do the people have to believe the company is going to look like in order to want to come to the company and make it truly great? [He explains:] Our people want to change the world; they want to know that the company is setting big, bold goals. We spend a great deal of time talking to our people, inspiring them on how we change the world.

Rather than just presenting the vision and values in written format, it is essential that they are communicated in a compelling and as participative a method as possible. In this way the vision and values come to life and people better understand the need for change. My consultancy has been involved in a large number of communications events around vision and values, ranging from individuals taking part in creative and participative activities to illustrate organizational vision and values, to senior managers each sponsoring an organizational value and endorsing best practice in bringing this to life.

Case studies

NCR

NCR is a global company that provides a range of products including enterprise data warehousing and retail systems. It employs 28,500 people worldwide. In 2005 NCR's CEO left the company after a 25-year tenure. The new CEO was Bill Nuti. His immediate challenge was to communicate the future direction of the company to its global workforce. He wanted, during his first 100 days, to disseminate the vision for the company going forward. To do this he met with employees, customers and investors on a global journey that took him to many countries. To keep employees informed and engaged in the process, NCR's communications team set up a special website that tracked his progress around the world. It included an 'Ask Bill' e-mail section where employees could e-mail questions about the vision directly to the new CEO. The communications team used the company's intranet and broadcast messages from Bill Nuti to reinforce the vision going forward.

Reuters

International technology company Reuters used an innovative approach to driving the need for change in its business. Hit by the stock market falls of the late 1990s, by the early 2000s Reuters had suffered severe financial losses and was loosing investor confidence. Recognizing the need for rapid change, the company established a change programme called 'Fast Forward'. Fast was an acronym for Reuter's new set of values that it believed would underpin the change process. These were 'fast, accountable, service-driven and team'. To communicate the new vision and values Reuters developed a two-stage programme.

The first stage was to engage the top 140 leaders from across the world in the development of the new strategy. A three-day strategy workshop was held in London which culminated in senior leaders being asked to show their confidence in the future of the company by buying shares. The value of these has since increased four-fold.

The next step was to communicate the new vision, values and strategy to the 15,000 employees in 140 countries across the world. Reuters set aside one day in 2003 when it held a global communications event for all its employees to mobilize them behind the change programme. Following the course of the sun and using high-tech in-house facilities, Reuters took employees in each country through a four-hour interactive session to inform them of the challenges and changes ahead. The sessions were led by country leaders, with supporting material supplied by the country team. They included a personal video message from the CEO, teleconferences and interactive sessions which were broadcast live to offices across the world. The overall impact was to mobilize and engage employees in the new vision and the need for change.

Key learning points

▌ Businesses can energize their workforces by providing a clear vision of the future direction of the company. This does not need to be a detailed 'what' or 'how' but a helicopter view of 'where' the company is headed that is presented in a motivational and inspirational way.

▌ Visions and values can come to life when they are communicating in a participative fashion so that employees have an opportunity to relate these to their day-to-day work and see 'what's in it for me'.

▌ Using innovative media can reinforce the message.

STRATEGIC GOALS

In addition to sharing the organization's vision, businesses, no matter in what sector, need to communicate clearly the organizational goals. The same applies with small as well as large organizations.

One example is Tower Homes, a London Housing association, which came top in the 2006 *Sunday Times* top 100 list of small companies to work for. As a charity, Tower Homes does not have shareholders, and the surpluses it generates go into providing more homes. The chief executive, Steve Walker, explained that being clear about the strategic direction the organization is taking has played a fundamental part in engaging staff. 'It has taken us years to create a culture where everyone is pointing in the right direction, is really clear about their role and has a positive attitude; the bottom line has improved accordingly', he says.

Walker claims that by focusing on clear goals, growth and productivity have increased every year, while costs have fallen. Staff turnover is 7 per cent, compared to an industry average of 16 per cent. 'That all comes from staff believing in what they do and wanting to be part of a great company', he says.

It is better to have fewer, more focused organizational goals that employees can relate to rather than a myriad of corporate objectives. Being clear what the goals are and constantly reinforcing them is key. If you asked people in your organization today what the strategic goals are, what would they say? Would they be able to relate these to the work they are undertaking and what their personal objectives and key result areas are?

Vodafone case study

Telecommunications giant Vodafone has six clear strategic goals that it communicates to all employees. In 2006 at the Institute of Directors annual conference in London, CEO Arin Sarun explained what that these are:

Goal number one is to delight our customers: we want to be even more customer-centric. We want to provide the best products and services in the mobile world.

The second goal is to build the best global team. We are a service business and we deliver our products and services through our employees. We need to make sure our employees are trained and are completely up to speed with what is going on in the world around them.

The third goal is leveraging scale and scope. Through a series of acquisitions, we have created the world's largest mobile communications company. We now need to harness this power. We operate in Japan, South Africa, America and all over Europe. How do we get the best ideas from around the world? How can we make sure that we pass them on to benefit our customers?

The fourth goal is expanding market boundaries both geographically and commercially. By going into eastern Europe, by getting into the entertainment business or the IT business, we are expanding the boundaries of our company and industry.

The fifth goal is providing a superior shareholder return. Through dividends, through share buybacks and through good resource allocation, we intend to make sure that we provide excellent rates of return.

The final goal is being a responsible business. This is not a luxury for us. Our products and services are intertwined with the fabric of society, and we have to take our responsibilities seriously.

Vodafone ensure that at every opportunity their leaders communicate these goals to their employees. Their view is that regularly reinforcing the vision, values and goals statements ensures that employees in the organization have the right big picture messages.

Key learning points

▌ Be clear about your strategic goals.

▌ It is better to have fewer, clear memorable strategic goals than, say, 20 unclear ones.

▌ Constantly remind employees of the strategic goals.

▌ Ensure that you relate the strategic goals to employees' specific key result areas.

KEEPING PEOPLE INFORMED

Several things that distinguish businesses that successfully communicate their vision, values and strategic goals to employees are:

▌ They use a variety of different communications media to get their message across in an interactive way.

▌ They encourage their executives to deliver the message in an approachable manner.

▌ They constantly reinforce the message.

USING DIFFERENT MEDIA

Take a sheet of paper and list all the methods there are to communicate to your workforce. These can range from conventional methods such as the intranet, team meetings, corporate newsletters or town hall meetings to banners in reception, lanyards and personal voice messages. Although one-to-one communication is important, there is a myriad of media that you can use to inform employees of key corporate goals and how they relate to individuals' jobs.

In the case of the optician retailer, the organization relied on managers' meetings and a half-yearly newsletter to disseminate information. Managers in turn were expected to hold team meetings in store, but shift patterns and part-time working meant that these often did not take place. At head office communication was slightly better with regular team briefings and use of notice boards.

INTERNAL COMMUNICATIONS DEPARTMENT

One of the key improvements that the optician retailer made was the creation of an internal communications department to help improve the information flow to employees. Reporting to the HR Director, they conducted a communications audit to assess the potential areas for improvement. The result was an action plan outlining the key messages that needed to be disseminated, the target audience and the best methodologies to be used.

If you have an internal communications department in place it can play a key role in promoting information flow. If you do not, do consider this as it is a worthwhile investment. A further consideration is to whom the head of internal communications should report. Typically the function sits within HR or marketing. Some organizations have the department reporting directly to the CEO or managing director in recognition of the vital role it plays.

MAKING INFORMATION INTERACTIVE AND CONTINUOUS

One of the roles that an internal communications department can take is to ensure that the information is presented in an interactive and participative fashion. Information is much more understandable and meaningful if there is an opportunity to ask questions and contribute ideas.

Look at television today and the degree of sophistication that there is in terms of how information is presented. This is the standard that employees will compare you to. As with television, employees need the ability to have constant news and information and also to see repeats, so remember to keep reinforcing and repeating the information.

Do not underestimate the powerful role that senior leaders can take in conveying information and engaging employees. The case studies below give examples of organizations that I have come across that have actively involved their senior leaders in the communications process. These examples should help you identify improvements in the area of information.

Volvo Group case study

In 2003 Volvo Group executives developed an employee engagement strategy that promoted strong employee involvement. This was branded 'The Volvo Way'.

Part of the strategy was to improve communication about, and involve employees more in, the attainment of the group's new strategic objectives. The business set a target of raising overall awareness of these from 67 per cent in 2002 to 80 per cent in 2005 as measured by its employee survey and it has exceeded these targets.

Volvo Group set up a network of communication representatives across each division. They were trained in how best to present the information to their colleagues given the diverse make-up and culture of each business unit. To support them in this task a website was set up linked to the company's intranet. Imagery was developed to represent each of the organization's strategic objectives; posters, Microsoft PowerPoint presentations and other material was developed to aid communication. In addition, the company's magazine and local newspapers were used to reinforce the message. The CEO was interviewed each month about one of the strategic objectives.

At a local level the communications representatives had freedom to communicate the objectives in the manner most relevant to their business. Various units produced their own material, workbooks and checklists to support the campaign. The board recognized that managers were the gatekeepers to disseminating information about the objectives. To ensure that this was done the CEO clearly set out his expectations of managers passing the information to the next level down, discussing the connections between local and global strategic objectives, and involving their teams in how these objectives could be achieved. All managers had to complete a report on what they had done. If they failed to respond they received a personal reminder from the CEO himself.

Key learning points

▌ Setting up local communications champions is a helpful way to disseminate business messages.

▌ The CEO can play a powerful role in reinforcing the expectations of managers to cascade information to their teams.

West Bromwich Building Society case study

Financial services organization West Bromwich Building Society has been running an employee engagement survey called the 'Factors employee commitment survey' for the past seven years. The survey measures various factors that contribute to employee engagement and allows the organization to benchmark itself against others. Two years ago the survey revealed a dip in its overall engagement score, particularly among sales staff. There had been a large number of new products introduced and the sales force had been subject to widespread reorganization. The survey revealed that staff were particularly critical of the style of communication from senior managers, which they perceived to be one way and non-inclusive.

To address this issue, the executive decided to hold a series of roadshows. Involving 30 to 40 people a day for two weeks, members of the executive headed by the CEO ran communication sessions with team members. The accent was on answering questions posed by staff and listening to their concerns. In particular, the executive answered questions about the future of the organization as well as explaining its aims and strategic goals. The listening process resulted in over 60 improvement points being raised and agreed as part of an overall action plan. In addition, the executive recognized the power of direct communication with team members. Each executive committed to organizing quarterly communications visits to dedicated areas to continue the listening process. Managers were also given training in adopting a more coaching leadership style to encourage involvement and feedback. In addition the organization changed its performance management system to focus more on the career aspirations of employees in the next three years.

Key learning point

Communication of an organization's vision and strategic goals becomes much more powerful when senior managers have direct interface with employees.

Chrysler case study

Motor manufacturer Chrysler uses two different forums to bring staff and senior business leaders together. One is 'Touchpoint' sessions with front-line staff where the senior communication teams meet to discuss topics raised by employees. The other forum came about as a result of feedback from some 'Touchpoint' sessions. Staff at these sessions said that they wanted direct contact with the senior management team. As a result 'For our information' (FOI) sessions have now been established. Here 60 people from a cross-section of employees are invited to a one-hour session with a member of the senior management team. During the first five minutes the senior manager gives a brief update on what's happening in the company. The rest of the hour is spent in a question and answer session where employees can ask whatever questions they like of the manager. These forums have been very successful in allowing employees to have face-to-face contact with the executive.

Key learning point

Executives should be prepared to answer questions to clarify the goals and to show that they are actively listening to employees.

Case studies

BT

In one division of telecommunications giant BT, research among employees highlighted the lack of visibility of its senior leader. As a result, people felt that they did not know what he stood for or was trying to achieve. Recognizing that it was important to share his vision for the business and strategy going forward, the senior executive began a series of videoed monthly briefings called 'What's on your mind'. The power of the videos lies in the process through which they are made. Every month one member of staff and one manager are selected at random to conduct an off-the-cuff interview with the senior executive where he or she shares views and reflections. The videos have been very well received by employees and have helped encourage more two-way conversations with the senior manager as he is now seen as more approachable.

AXA Insurance

At AXA Insurance the Chief Executive produces a fortnightly audio message for all employees as a communications update about the business. Team members and managers are encouraged to e-mail their thoughts and questions about his messages. They then receive a personal reply.

The UK Police Force

In the United Kingdom, senior leaders in the police force are also adopting a more informal approach to communication, with several chief constables developing their own daily blogs, which have proved very successful.

General Motors

At General Motors vice chairman and CEO Bob Lutz's blog site has attracted continuous attention from employees and received a huge amount of feedback – both positive and negative. The overall feeling is that the blog has done a lot to create a feeling of a personal relationship with the top of the organization and has put a face to the organization's senior leader.

Manpower

In order to support the launch of its new values, the senior management team at workforce provider Manpower organized a different postcard to be sent each day to all its employees to communicate the new organizational values. This was accompanied by a small gift. So, for example, for the value 'Fresh thinking' it sent a card saying: 'How can you freshen up your ideas and challenge the norm?' This was accompanied by a gift of peppermints for all employees.

Pitney Bowes

When Pitney Bowes introduced a transformational change programme for its business, key to the success was the constant reinforcement of the message for change. The CEO set up a weekly 'power talk' via a voicemail message to employees. This was a series of different motivational messages linked to the new vision for the future.

Mayo Clinic

At award winning medical centre Mayo Clinic in the United States, leaders' messages are posted on a special intranet site called 'Leadership Perspectives'. This reinforces the vision of the organization and its key strategic goals. It also provides employees with access to leaders' personal thoughts on business issues, including customer service and company culture. The Clinic has reviewed its communications medium to ensure that it provides a variety of methods to suit different target groups. These include e-screens, bulletin boards and online news. It revamped its newsletter so that there is now a hard copy version, an e-version and an e-mail summary for those people who only want to see the headlines.

Hallmark

At Hallmark Cards the CEO finds time to speak regularly at induction sessions for all new starters. He communicates the company's vision and strategic goals and takes part in a question and answer session.

Ritz Carlton

Hotel chain Ritz Carlton has 'line-ups' where all 22,000 staff have a meeting with their supervisor, manager, the vice president or chief executive of their location at the start of their shift. They spend 15 minutes covering essential items, ranging from which VIPs are staying in the hotel that day to staff suggestions. Everyone across the world discusses the same subject every day – one of the 20 basics taken in turn. Some of these basics include:

▌ It is the responsibility of each staff member to create a work environment of teamwork and (seamless) lateral service so that the needs of our guests and each other are met every day.

▌ When a guest has a special need or has a problem, staff members should break away from their normal duties and resolve the issue. Each staff member is empowered (with up to US $2,000 per incident).

Federal Express

Federal Express has its own television station so that the CEO can talk to all of the employees worldwide. He will also answer unprompted questions live.

Key learning points

▌ Senior managers can be seen as more approachable and send out positive messages when they engage in regular communication channels with employees.

▌ Use a range of different media to make senior managers more accessible to employees.

▌ Allow staff members opportunity to question senior leaders so that they better understand the business rationale.

▌ Re-evaluate your communication vehicles. What has worked in the past may need refreshing and updating. Electronic media such as blogs, e-mail and intranets are growing in importance and encourage instant feedback from employees.

▌ Do not rely on one event or activity; communication about the company's vision and goals should be constant.

BEST PRACTICE IN INTERNAL COMMUNICATIONS

To encourage involvement, here are some practical things that organizations should do:

▌ Have a system of regular briefings and consultation to keep employees informed of market trends, trading performance, business developments, emerging issues and changes.

▌ Use as many relevant channels as possible. These could include town hall meetings, team and one-to-one briefings, notice boards, internal e-mail, intranet, employee annual reports, newsletters, corporate video and business television. Don't miss out remote workers such as part-time workers, people working from home or sales people who may be travelling a lot.

▌ Build in feedback mechanisms and respond to feedback. This shows concern, involvement and shared ownership of issues.

▌ Where significant changes are under consideration, take time to explain the background and why this is important to the business and to those affected. Don't keep people in the dark. This will only allow rumour to spread and issues to become exaggerated. Constantly reinforce the messages and allow time for questions and reactions.

▌ Be honest. People appreciate plain speaking and if they feel that you are only telling part of the story, confidence will be undermined.

▌ Be consistent. Ensure that internal briefings and public communication are consistent.

▌ Create communications champions. Acknowledge people who role model the behaviours that you would like to encourage, such as making positive suggestions and providing constructive feedback.

Great Little Box Company case study

The Great Little Box Company employs 200 workers. As its name implies, the company produces cartons and boxes. A Canadian company, it has won several awards for people management, including appearing in a list of in Canada's top 100 employers for 2007. The company has undertaken many improvement initiatives to help increase the levels of employee engagement.

On the communication front, the organization recognizes the importance of using different forms of media to keep employees fully informed. 'We used to have a yearly strategy plan meeting', explains the CEO Robert Meggy on the Industry Canada website. 'Everyone would get all excited for a few days and them they'd forget about everything we talked about.' Instead the company now has five different meetings chaired by five different people around specific agenda items: one for cost decrease, one for sales increase, one for customer service, one for SWOT and long-term planning, one for employee well-being. This encourages employees to come up with ideas for improvement and has helped motivation and sales growth. In addition, each member of staff has a one-to-one review session with their supervisor or line manager on a quarterly basis. This covers these questions:

▮ How are we doing?

▮ How are you doing personally?

▮ What can we do to help you?

▮ How am I doing as your supervisor?

In addition, each employee has a yearly review where they discuss their 5- to 10-year goals, irrespective of whether it has anything to do with the company.

The company is run on an open book policy with everyone being made aware of the financial performance. This, cites Meggy, is helpful in ensuring that employees relate to the future of the business. To create a sense of trust around reporting, senior managers take time to explain financial accounts. The company has a monthly profit-sharing programme which is equal across the board. If the company achieves a particular stretch goal, all employees in the company enjoy an all-inclusive weekend trip to an exciting destination.

The company promotes regularly from within and has an employee of the month programme. Every month one winner is announced who receives a prize and a parking space for the month at the front of the building. Runners-up get gift certificates.

'Do you care about the future of the company?' receives the most positive response in the company's annual survey.

Key learning points

▌ Less is more. Consider holding separate communications meetings to inform employees about individual strategic goals.

▌ Make sure that there is a link between the organization's strategic objectives and individuals' performance goals.

▌ Provide training to employees in how to read financial statements.

PERSONAL PRESENCE AND IMPACT

Do not forget the power of personal presence and impact. Messages often get lost if the messenger is weak and insignificant. It is imperative that senior managers receive personal coaching and development in presentation and communication skills. Likewise my advice is that all managers receive similar training in order to motivate and inspire others. Making people aware of their own style of communication and their own preferences is a first step.

Typically people have a preference for one of four basic styles of communication. At times they may use a combination of two styles:

Direct

The person:

▌ takes charge;

▌ communicates directly;

▌ is assertive;

▌ focuses on the big picture.

Engaging

The person is:

▌ persuasive;

▌ energetic;

▌ enthusiastic;

▌ spontaneous.

Systematic

The person is:

▌ focused on detail;

▌ analytical;

▌ methodical;

▌ thorough.

Cohesive

The person:

▌ is considerate;

▌ actively listens;

▌ is collaborative;

▌ is patient.

The challenge for communicators is to adapt their style to the target audience. People who are engaging, for example, may get impatient and 'switch off' if they are presented material in a very systematic manner.

HELPING SENIOR LEADERS TO IMPROVE THEIR COMMUNICATION STYLE

The HR director of the optician retailer was keen that the CEO and the senior leadership team inform staff directly of the organization's new vision and strategic goals. She organized a series of roadshows for the senior leadership team. A video was also made of the CEO talking about the future of the organization.

The problem was that the CEO in particular was fairly wooden in his communication style. A natural introvert and good with figures, his message missed the mark as it lacked enthusiasm in its delivery. In the initial video briefing employee feedback centred on the lack of congruence of the message rather than the vision itself. With some personal coaching the CEO adapted his style so that he appeared more enthusiastic and inspiring to employees.

As an HR professional or change agent, a key role that you can play in increasing employee engagement scores for information is to help senior managers improve their communications style. This clearly needs to be done in a sensitive manner, but via careful coaching and support, senior leadership teams can improve their style.

Case studies

Agilent Technologies

At Agilent Technologies, for example, great effort has been placed on helping the 150 top leaders to communicate effectively with their team. Each leader has a 'communications counsellor', one of the communications team who attends some of their meetings and provides feedback on the impact of their communication style.

Mayo Clinic

At Mayo Clinic, in the United States, the communications team has worked with senior managers to help them best communicate the organization's vision. The team has created a personal communications plan for each of its senior managers. Each leader meets on a regular basis with a script writer who helps craft key messages for employees. Recognizing the power of storytelling to convey powerful messages they also use the services of a storyteller who helps them personalize the messages they convey.

Barclays Bank

Barclays Bank put 6,000 of its leaders over an 18-month period through a transformational leadership programme designed to make the bank more customer focused. Each week a member of the senior leadership team attended the programme to speak to the 25–100 leaders who were going through the course at one time. Their brief was to make the vision and objectives of the company come alive in a motivational way for employees. With the help of some personal coaching each leader conveyed the vision and related their personal story of what this meant for them. The self-revelation and personalization of the communication had a powerful effect on the audience, who left highly energized and motivated by the way the message had been conveyed.

Key learning points

▌ Offer feedback, coaching and support to senior managers to help them convey a meaningful message.

▌ Use the services of professional communications consultants and script writers to sharpen your leaders' messages.

Checklist

How does your organization inform employees in a motivating way about the business's vision and strategic objectives?

Use this checklist to evaluate the methods your organization uses to inform employees about its vision and strategic goals.

Criteria	In place	Not applicable	Needs to be actioned or addressed
The organization has a clear vision of the future			
The organizational vision is well communicated across the company			
Senior leaders describe the organizational vision in a motivational way			
The organization has a clear set of strategic goals			
The strategic goals are known and understood by employees			
The organization has a clear set of organizational values that are well communicated			
The organization's vision and strategic goals are constantly communicated and reinforced			
The organization uses a variety of methods to communicate the organizational vision, values and goals			

The second letter of WIFI stands for information. This chapter has focused on the need for clarity around organizational vision, values and goals, which is essential in helping the employee to know where they are going and why and how they fit into these elements. The regularity and appropriateness of information at all levels is a key driver of engagement. Senior managers play a pivotal role in this process. The next chapter addresses the issue of fairness.

7

Fairness

The third letter of WIFI stands for fairness. This can be seen in many aspects of the employee journey, starting with recruitment and selection. Hiring the right people for the right jobs is fundamental to ensuring that individuals begin their working life with your organization in the most positive way.

Fairness also manifests itself in the performance management process your business adopts. Being clear about what is expected of people in their job and receiving regular and timely motivational and developmental feedback appear as key factors in all research on employee engagement. Likewise, it has been established that it is important for employees to have a personal development plan. Ready access to training and development that meets individual needs has been proven to be important for many organizations in developing a culture of engagement. Finally, businesses with high levels of employee engagement provide appropriate and fair reward and recognition.

This chapter looks at the issue of fairness. It outlines the principles that lead to a sense of fairness in an organization. It also looks at the levers that businesses can pull to increase the perception of fairness in their organization.

RESPECTING THE INDIVIDUAL

Believing that you are being dealt with in a fair manner leads to a climate of openness and respect. Treating employees fairly is about making sure that every aspect of the employee journey is based on best practice, so that if the employee looks outside the organization to compare it with other businesses, they will see that they are being treated fairly and with respect. Fairness manifests itself in business practices such as those shown in Figure 7.1.

Perhaps your organization already has all these practices in place. The key is what your employees tell you about them and where improvements can be made.

For example, in the case of the optician retailer, employees scored the learning and development opportunities highly (the retailer had invested in a comprehensive programme of development). However, they felt that the recruitment and selection process was unfair and that there was little opportunity for career development.

RECRUITMENT AND SELECTION

Organizations that are 'best in class' have a robust process for recruitment and selection. One of the problems that employees who worked for the optician retailer highlighted was the perception that jobs were not always advertised internally and that even when they were, many of the vacancies had already been filled before the advert was placed. The recruitment and selection process was viewed as just a front.

Organizations who have 'best in class' recruitment and selection processes appear to be very clear about the type of people they wish to

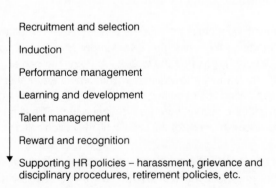

Recruitment and selection

Induction

Performance management

Learning and development

Talent management

Reward and recognition

Supporting HR policies – harassment, grievance and disciplinary procedures, retirement policies, etc.

Figure 7.1   The employee journey

attract and about the recruitment and selection process itself. An example is Southwest Airlines, which has become infamous for recruiting for attitude and then training for skills. The company has over 2,000 applications for every one vacant position. In the United Kingdom, First Direct has a pre-screening process on its website. It is a multiple choice questionnaire. The results tell the candidate and the company how well the person matches the culture and values of the organization. If there is not a match, then candidates are thanked and encouraged to look elsewhere.

Mobile phone retailer Carphone Warehouse adopts a similar approach. The company places great importance on recruiting and developing the right people. Speaking to the magazine *Customer Management* in March 2006, the HR director explained:

> You need to make sure that if you are hiring on skill and attitude, you invest in your people to make that happen. In our shops, nobody is put in front of a customer until they have had two weeks training here. Everyone who goes through that programme is tested, not in the authoritarian sense, but on the basis that if you don't pass the test, maybe you are in the wrong job.

It is important that employees genuinely buy in to the culture. In his interview, the HR director of Carphone Warehouse continued:

> It starts off with wanting to be an employer of choice. We want people to work for us because they want to work for us, not because it happens to be the next job on the list. It you've got that, the recruitment stage should be a lot easier because the people that respond to your ads, on the web – where we do loads of recruitment – or on the recruitment hotline, they are already in the value set that you want.

The company believes that having an open company ethos is a large factor in ensuring buy-in to company culture at all levels:

> We measure it, we recruit to it, which is very important. When we promote, we take it through the ranks, that's very important. There's no secret, all company feedback goes on the website and anyone can access it. I do think that you can use it to evaluate management and if there's an area where over a period you're getting a trend in certain aspects, which are not in tandem with the culture, you have to deal with it. This is quite a strong culture so if it doesn't work for the individual, they often self-select out.

The benefits of a values-based approach to recruitment and selection are also evident at engineering firm Arup. Employee attrition rates run at 12 per cent as compared to 20 per cent for the industry as a whole. The business attributes this to the 'spiritual employment contract' that it develops with the workforce. Owned by three trusts, the organization has a profit-sharing scheme which means everyone is a shareholder. Its recruitment and selection process is geared to hiring graduates who are attracted by the organization's values, ethics and social consciousness. Typically the people the company employs are mavericks with an eye for creativity. The company has a strong performance management culture. It also encourages global networking and knowledge sharing.

There is a trend therefore to using desired values and behaviours as a screening mechanism in best practice organizations. Other businesses develop a profile of their best performers and recruit against these characteristics. Others again use psychometric profiling and assessment centre techniques to ensure that they are attracting and hiring the right people.

Assessment centres and behavioural interviewing

Organizations need to consider the best ways of providing a fair, objective and accurate means of assessing candidates' knowledge, skills and abilities. Applicants must be considered equally on merit at each stage of the recruitment process. Selection must be based on relevant criteria applied consistently to all candidates. One way to avoid bias is to ensure that a range of selection methods is used for recruitment. Interview is one of the least reliable methods of recruitment, so it is important that this is part of the process not just the sole method.

Organizations are increasingly relying on assessment centres to gain evidence of potential employees' behaviours. Here candidates undertake a variety of exercises to demonstrate their skills, knowledge and behaviour. If your organization uses interviews as a selection method do ensure that people are trained to use behavioural-based interview questions.

Most interviews contain questions where the interviewer puts forward a situation and asks the applicant theoretical questions about how they would deal with it. The interviewer may get an excellent answer. However, all this is telling the interviewer is that the person knows what they *should* do, not whether they are likely to do it! Similarly, some people may not know the textbook response but may, when faced with a real-life situation, respond appropriately with successful results.

Behavioural-based interview questions ask for specific examples of situations that have required the person to demonstrate a specific quality. For example: 'Tell me about a particularly difficult customer you've dealt with and how you won them round.' By doing this you focus on the actual behaviour demonstrated by the applicant. This is a fairer and more robust method of interviewing.

Likewise, do not forget to give feedback to successful and unsuccessful candidates. In an effort to improve the fairness of its recruitment and selection policy, London Underground has adopted a policy of giving feedback to all candidates who apply for a job. This has helped the organization to ensure that it is making recruitment decisions based on objective criteria.

INDUCTION

It is important that new recruits are given a thorough induction to the workplace. This is a great opportunity to inform employees of the vision and goals of the organization and to share its values. One of my colleagues always reminds me of the importance of this when she recounts the story of the induction into her former company. Unfortunately, she was thrown straight into the job and her formal induction did not begin for another four months. By the end of the first four months, having worked with a team with a high number of cynics, her attitude towards the organization had turned from one of bright enthusiasm to sourness and disillusionment.

Best practice organizations such as the National Heritage Lottery and Department of Media, Culture and Sport adopt a blended approach to induction where new recruits undertake discovery activities, use e-learning, attend workshops and are mentored by their manager.

Key learning points

▌ Make sure that you have a robust selection and recruitment process that is linked to your organizational values.

▌ Advertise jobs internally and make sure that the selection criteria are clear.

▌ Offer feedback to all candidates whether they have been successful or not.

▌ Check that your induction process is sending the right messages to new recruits – it is the first 100 days that make or break people's perception of the organization.

PERFORMANCE MANAGEMENT

An essential aspect of fairness is knowing personally what you are doing well in terms of your performance and where you can develop. According to a recent survey by the Chartered Institute of Personnel and Development, one-third of workers in the United Kingdom never get any feedback on their performance, two-fifths are not told what their career prospects are.

Holding performance reviews is a basic requirement of all managers, but many still see this as a chore and, as the research shows, do not review performance at all. At the optician retailer there was a haphazard approach to performance appraisal. Some branch staff took part in annual appraisals, others did not. Some branch managers were appraised, others not, and so on up the chain. This is a leadership issue. If senior managers do not take the time to review their managers' performance, they do not set a positive role model for others to do this. If one-to-one time with the manager is not built into everyone's diary, performance quickly drifts and motivation levels fall.

Some organizations have created processes to encourage managers to hold regular reviews.

Case studies

AXA

When insurance group AXA introduced a new performance management system several years ago, it made it part of managers' objectives to hold four performance reviews with their staff each year. As the attainment of managers' objectives was linked to their bonus awards, there was a powerful incentive to achieve this.

TAP Pharmaceuticals

At TAP Pharmaceuticals, which employs 3,000 people in the United States, to ensure that managers provide regular feedback and coaching to their employees managers are given an incentive for completing team members' performance reviews. These are linked to pay and if the manager does not submit the performance review on time, neither the manager nor the team member will receive an increase until it is completed. Once the review is completed the team member receives his or her merit pay backdated to the appropriate date. The manager, however, receives his or her merit increase from the next payroll date and not backdated.

Key learning points

▌ Build into managers' objectives the need to hold regular performance reviews with their staff.

▌ Consider penalties for non-completion of reviews.

REVIEWING THE 'WHAT' AND THE 'HOW'

A further trend in terms of performance management is to measure the behaviours or competencies of individuals as well as how well they achieve their objectives. This process allows individuals to receive feedback not just on what they have achieved but also how they did this. Developed as a concept by GE, the idea is that this process aligns people to the desired organizational values and behaviours. Individuals may, for example, achieve all their objectives but do so in way which is completely counter-cultural, so reviewing their competencies and behaviours provides a more balanced approach.

Lack of achievement of organizational goals and lack of demonstration of the desired behaviours equates to poor performance. If individuals achieve their objectives but their behaviours are at odds with those desired in their role, there is potential misalignment between the organization and the individual. If individuals do not achieve their objectives but demonstrate the desired organizational behaviours, they should be given a second chance. With coaching and support they should be able to demonstrate improvements. The peak performer is the person who both achieves his or her objectives and demonstrates organizational behaviours. This is illustrated in Figure 7.2.

A lot of debate surrounds whether performance should be linked to pay. Reward is important, although it is not by all means the only factor that keeps people with the organization. In order to be fair to employees, businesses need to consider where they would like to sit in terms of reward in relation to other organizations in their sector. Best practice is to benchmark your organization's performance management and reward system against other people in your sector. This will allow you to consider whether your system is fair.

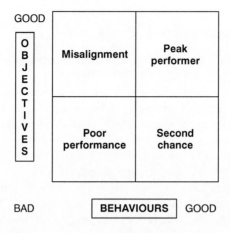

Figure 7.2 The objectives and behaviours matrix

LEARNING AND DEVELOPMENT

Another characteristic of organizations with high levels of engagement is that employees are asked what training they want (rather than forced into something that may not help) and their transferable skills are improved. They also receive a considerable amount of training. For example, in the United States retailer The Container Store, which continually tops the polls for customer and employee engagement, offers each of its 1,300 employees 135 hours of training per year. After 10 years all employees receive a sabbatical.

Part of the challenge of the manager in helping individuals to identify learning and development opportunities is creating an understanding that learning is not just restricted to training courses. For example, development may also take place on the job. There are a range of learning and development options open to individuals – self-study, e-learning, seminars, conferences and workshops, coaching and mentoring, to name but a few – all of which, according to the need, may support individuals in acquiring new skills and knowledge, changing behaviours and keeping abreast of developments in their areas of work.

Development interventions should be tailored to the needs and the learning styles of individual team members. Team development may offer opportunities for enhancing team work and better understanding across the group. The learning and development professional therefore needs to balance the needs of individual development with group-wide requirements.

BUPA Care Homes case study

Faced with a decline in client satisfaction, BUPA Care Homes implemented a series of practical training sessions in 2004. These were reinforced by a video presentation specially designed to give employees an insight into what it was like to be a frail, elderly resident in one of the company's 298 homes.

Among other activities, employees took turns to act the part of residents and be fed or lifted by their colleagues. This exercise led to procedural changes and made staff more empathetic with their clients.

The organization had a clear strategic agenda to improve customer care and it aligned everything to that – with a long-term, not a quick-fix, perspective. The programme was designed to cover all 25,000 UK staff and managers, with adaptations for non-client-facing employees. It has since been extended into an award scheme and continuous quality improvement process. It is now used to induct new recruits and is about to be extended to BUPA's care homes in Spain.

Residents' satisfaction scores are now at their highest level. Job satisfaction scores are also the highest and 2005 saw the best-ever financial results for BUPA Care Homes – 25 per cent better than the previous year.

The scheme also directly engaged line managers and was flexible enough to suit the needs of different locations. This part of BUPA turned its business around by involving its people and securing their commitment to improved client care.

Key learning point

There is power in every member of staff having a joint shared development experience.

Nationwide Building Society case study

Nationwide is a major player in the banking, mortgage and insurance markets, with more than 15,000 employees spread across 700 offices in the United Kingdom. In terms of staff development, the society has introduced measures to standardize practices across the whole group, including 360-degree appraisals and a passport system for those new to the organization. Everyone gets a passport. As they move through the organization, the passport will be signed by line managers when it has been established that the holder understands what is going on in a particular division.

All divisions in the Nationwide group follow a three-stage approach to performance reviews, involving an assessment of what a particular member of staff is required to do, an agreed set of development targets and a strategy to improve performance. Within this framework, each business unit then has to devise techniques to assess the effectiveness of the measures taken.

While the various business divisions have a certain amount of autonomy in terms of how they manage and develop staff, a team of divisional co-ordinators has been appointed to identify practices that could be used successfully in other parts of the organization.

When Nationwide was awarded Investors in People Champions status in 2004, it committed itself to sharing best practice with other organizations through open days and mentoring schemes. In this way the society is not only imparting information but learning from others too.

Key learning points

▌ Ensure that development needs and opportunities are discussed as part of a performance review.

▌ Instigate a system for recording development needs and attainment.

▌ Benchmark your development against best practice.

There are many organizations that believe that *any* development is good for engagement. Some examples appear in the following case studies.

Case studies

Wawa

One way that Wawa, a US retailer that operates more than 500 stores in five eastern states, has created high levels of engagement, even in a minimum wage business, is to offer free tuition fees at three colleges with which it has relationships. It encourages employees to enrol on any degree course that they would like on the basis that any education not only benefits the individual but the company and the community. In addition, Wawa offers an in-house suite of 100 training programmes that are open to all employees.

St Luke's

Every year, London-based advertising agency St Luke's gives every member of staff £150 to spend on making themselves more interesting. The rules are simple: it has to be something you want to do, not something you have to do – so tuba lessons count, driving lessons don't. It has to give you a new and permanent skill – so learning Mongolian counts, going there doesn't.

All staff must provide two pieces of evidence of what they have done with their £150 – something to go on the office wall such as a certificate, and a demonstration of their new found talent at a staff meeting. They can choose to add together two years' worth of money, but if they fail to use the money for more than two years in a row then they will no longer be eligible for the scheme. The philosophy is, if you've done nothing of interest in two years then you are boring beyond help.

All new joiners are also given £100 to buy the agency a present. It means that they have to get to know the people they work with and get under the skin of the agency culture to find something appropriate which is then delivered at an informal agency meeting. Presents have included an aquarium, a karaoke machine and some hamsters.

St Luke's was created as a cooperative in 1996 and although its structure has changed over the years, its ideas to keep staff happy and motivated are still as radical as when it first started. There is a board consisting of four members which runs the agency with some external expertise brought in to provide a wider business perspective. However, the decisions made by the board can be and have been challenged by the Quest group – six employees who are voted for annually by employees.

The agency came second in the 2004 *Sunday Times* league of the 50 best smaller companies to work for. When surveyed, 90 per cent of its staff said they loved working there and 94 per cent were proud of the company, while 71 per cent said they had found their dream job – the highest score in the *Sunday Times* survey.

Among the perks are an on-site café which offers a free breakfast, subsidized lunch and free refreshments. And to help people think creatively, there are regular trips to galleries and artists are invited to bring their work in. If a creative says 'I'd really like to go on a comedy course' or something, that's fine, they can go out and do that. The important point here is that all learning is valued and efforts are made to introduce opportunities for it whenever we can in order to enhance their skills.

QuikTrip

The US-based convenience store chain QuikTrip (QT) is a privately owned company that operates over 400 convenience stores in the Unite States. It has a turnover of US $4 billion and its shares have risen during the same period at over four times the S & P rate. QT has been listed in the Fortune 100 best places to work three years in a row. Feedback in customer surveys highlights two things that customers believe are unique to the brand: the people who work in the stores seem glad to be there and they seem to like customers and their teammates.

QT's success is partly down to the rigorous recruitment and selection process that it adopts. It has a clear vision of the skills and characteristics of a successful QT employee. These include hiring people who like people, are patient and are extrovert. It puts candidates through a structured recruitment process that benchmarks candidates against successful current employees. The assessment process includes a personality assessment followed by interviews designed to probe for evidence of desired behaviours. The company has eight geographic regions and, to maintain a consistent approach to recruitment and selection, a manager from each region handles the hiring.

A further characteristic that distinguishes QT is the amount of training that it offers all new employees. Each new member of staff is partnered with a personal trainer from the regional hiring office who acts as a buddy and mentor to the new recruit for the first two weeks. They work at the store with the new recruit and help induct them into the way of working and QT culture.

QT has a philosophy of promoting from within. All of its over 400 store managers worked their way through the ranks, as did the majority of its executives. This creates a strong feeling of teamwork and trust among employees. In addition, although pay is on a par with the company's competitors, QT offers a generous benefits package. This includes 10–25 days' holiday entitlement, 10 days of sick pay, an option to purchase two further weeks' holiday and 10 additional days off without pay to attend family and personal events. This package is very unusual in the US retail sector, where the average entitlement is 10 days' holiday.

QT is very open with its associates about the company performance and its long-term strategy. It trains all its employees to read their store's monthly financial statements and each associate earns a bonus that is linked to the store's operating profit. It also allocates 5 per cent of its annual net profits to charity.

Key learning points

▌ Encouraging lifelong learning is a powerful weapon in engagement, as is offering ample amounts of training.

▌ Organizations such as QT and St Luke's challenge the traditional approach to learning and development.

Finally in this section on learning and development, it is worth emphasizing that HR professionals' challenge is to position learning and development as an investment not a cost to the business. Best practice is for everyone from senior managers downward to have a personal development plan and to undertake personal development regularly.

One organization that has successfully funded a suite of learning and development programmes as well as developing links with the local community is Panasonic. It jointly hosts learning events with local businesses. These pay to send people on the programmes at a subsidized rate. In this way both Panasonic and the local businesses benefit as there are more delegates on the programme and therefore a greater chance of the programmes going ahead in a cost-effective way.

CAREER DEVELOPMENT AND SUCCESSION PLANNING

Increasing the type and quantity of training opportunities helps engagement. Another area of importance in the area of fairness is career development and succession planning. In the example of the optician retailer I dealt with, it was difficult for people to have line of sight from the bottom to the top of the organization. Opportunities for promotion and advancement were perceived to be very few. In addition, there was not much prospect for employees of lateral career moves due to location constraints and the silo nature of the organizational structure. To make career development even less easy, the company had also issued an edict that employees needed to stay in their roles for at least two years before they could apply for another job. They then had to be referred for this by their manager. Something had to change!

One of the areas that I find can be a key lever to higher levels of engagement in an organization is providing opportunities for progression. This doesn't just mean upwards progression. Many people are happy with the level they are in the organization but may want to make lateral moves.

A lot of emphasis today is put on talent management in an organization. My view is that this is important, but having fair career development opportunities for all is equally so. Employees should know that the company values lateral experience as well as upward promotion. Providing multiple career path models will open up horizons for employees. For those that show potential there should also be a talent management programme.

TALENT MANAGEMENT

To ensure that employees are treated fairly, employees need to see that if they display talent and have potential, there are opportunities for them to progress.

Relatively low unemployment across the economy as a whole and the need for continued growth means that organizations increasingly have to compete for potential employees. Attracting, retaining and developing talented people, therefore, is crucial. Indeed, a recent survey attracting and retaining skilled employees was deemed to be the highest 'risk' to employers. European client studies carried out by accountancy firm Grant Thornton indicate that the cost of recruitment averages around £30,000 a head, so being able to reduce those costs through better retention will in itself lead to considerable savings. In the future they predict that there will be acute talent shortages in the areas of customer service, health care, computer support and technology.

In emerging economies, there is also a shortage of talent. China's enormous population, for example, belies the fact that less than 10 per cent of China's university graduates (estimated at more than 4 million in 2006) have the skills required to become leaders of global businesses. The easy option in countries like India, China and Brazil has been to increase the pay levels of the most desirable employees and inflate their job titles. However, this will only buy loyalty for a limited period. Training and development as well as talent management programmes are equally important as pay and benefits.

In India and China supply of local leaders is seriously limited, creating severe competition for talent. For example, Shanghai and Bangalore have turnover rates in some sectors that are greater than 40 per cent per year. As a result, salary inflation is also significant with salary levels of some talented individuals becoming equal to or greater than their counterparts in London or Singapore. One leading automotive company in China, for example, increased the levels of engagement and sales performance of its sales people by instigating a talent management programme focusing on targeted development interventions as well as overseas rotations and a stratified reward strategy.

The challenge for China and India will also be to reverse the 'brain drain' effect that has happened in these countries in the past and to encourage educated nationals to return. They will compete for talent on the global market with countries such as the United States, where 22 per cent of science and engineering positions are now held by foreign nationals (up from 14 per cent in 1990). Firms in the Asia-Pacific believe that home-grown executives can have a greater impact on company performance than expatriates and are seeking to accelerate their talent development programmes.

Organizations are therefore increasingly focusing on talent management and are moving from a reactive to a proactive approach. There are various stages in developing a talent management strategy. Firstly, there is gaining buy-in from the CEO – without this a talent management programme will fail. The CEO and the board will need to take an active role in promoting the scheme, acting as mentors, participating in talent reviews and succession-planning activities. Secondly, there is deciding on and publicizing the criteria for the scheme, and thirdly using the criteria to identify talent.

Various assessment tools and techniques that focus not only on performance but also on potential can help here. Once people are on the programme, organizations need to ensure that these people have appropriate development opportunities. These can include job rotations, access to senior leadership, coaching and mentoring, special projects and additional support. Succession plans then need to be in place to provide a clear view of how the development of the high-potential group will lead to the fulfilment of net generation leadership roles.

Organizations from the Civil Service through to private sector businesses have developed their own definitions of what are talent and potential. Equally there are a wide range of methods that people use, from development centres through to links to performance ratings, line manager nominations and psychometric testing.

One definition of high potential is the employee's ability to make two vertical moves in an organization within four years. A model developed by London Business School defines the characteristics of high-potential employees as:

▌ intellect: having high IQ, 'horsepower', ability to be analytical, ability to synthesize information;

▌ energy: having the motivation to do it themselves, dedication, willingness to take risks, willingness to take on more;

▌ creativity: being proactive, seeking out new information, having a desire to learn, being comfortable with ambiguity, seeing value in change;

▌ charisma: having emotional intelligence, demonstrating spiritual intelligence, being an inspiration and motivation to others.

Different organizations take different approaches to talent management. At Unilever, for example, the approach is to say to people: you're part of a pool of people who have high potential, and there will be competition in that pool. It makes the culture more competitive than if you simply say: "You'll get a promotion after a certain amount of time."'

At Standard Chartered the bank's policy is not to say who the high potential people are. 'If you tell your high potentials it raises their expectations. I don't think that our line managers are at a state where they can manage people's expectations if we tell them.'

At global cosmetics company Avon, a new talent management system was developed to shift the emphasis away from a line manager referral system, where managers recommended staff for promotion, to an objective and more formal approach using a leadership model to better determine suitability for various roles. It also uses a database to identify where talent lies in the organization.

Home appliance maker Whirlpool Corporation has adopted a positive discrimination approach to talent management by targeting women to go on the programme. This is because this group is under-represented among their management population.

Whatever your approach (and I personally believe that it is best for people to know where they are), research shows that top talent is attracted to and motivated to stay with a business when:

▌ The work is interesting and challenging.

▌ There are development opportunities.

▌ Talented employees have a manager or mentor they admire.

▌ There are opportunities to engage with senior management and respected mentors.

▌ High performers are recruited and looked after.

▌ There is a long-term commitment to top talent.

▌ The company has a good reputation and is a strong performer.

▌ The company will look good on a CV.

▌ Culture and values are aligned to the high performers' own.

▌ There is trust in senior management.

▌ Talented people are recognized and rewarded for their individual and team contribution.

Most organizations now recognize the need to develop talent management programmes to identify potential and to provide development opportunities for talented people across the organization. Here are some examples of the types of activities that people undertake.

Case studies

UBS

In 2004 financial services organization UBS launched the first group-wide high-potential programme, the 'Accelerated Leadership Experience'. The development of high-potential employees happens first at divisional level and then, as they get more senior, within the group-wide accelerated leadership experience. Individuals who are selected for the group-wide programme spend a couple of months working with a learning partner from HR on a number of areas, including personality assessment, career development and the identification of a specific business challenge.

They then attend a three-and-a-half day intensive programme with their learning partner. This looks at three core elements: How do I understand and 'leverage' what is going on across the organization? How do I focus more effectively on clients? And how can I make myself a better leader?

After that, a personalized development plan for the next year is set out and individuals begin to work with a mentor from another part of the business. Alumni events – with input from both internal and external speakers – are also organized to keep high potentials updated and provide networking opportunities.

Aetna

Aetna is a diversified US company offering health care, dental, pharmacy, group life, disability and long-care insurance and employee benefits. It has participation rates of 90 per cent in its engagement surveys.

One area it identified for improvement as a result of the surveys was talent management. Its vision was to build talent that was not only deep but also broad so everyone in the company could develop. It realized that this new approach to talent management represented a significant cultural shift. Some managers were apprehensive in that adopting a universal system that identified talent in each part of the business, 'talent' in their own area would be lost to other parts of the business. Part of the challenge in making the new system work was shifting the mindset to Aetna talent rather than the talent in their area. Aetna set up a talent management system that can be accessed online. The concept is that any part of the business can draw on the central talent pool.

Sony Europe

Another organization that takes a different approach to talent management is Sony Europe, which has developed a programme called 'The Strengths Way'. Part of the Sony Corporation's founding principle is that the environment be a place where 'technical personnel of sincere motivation can exercise their abilities to the maximum'. Its philosophy towards development is to focus on people's strengths. So, for example, in the performance review process people spend time analysing the competencies in which they are strongest and seeing how they apply them to their current role. The organization has developed a mentoring scheme for graduates, high-potential employees, executives and executive successors. This scheme has been designed to focus on people's strengths and how they can be applied in the workplace. The success of the mentoring scheme has been that each mentor group becomes a mentor to the next. In addition, the business has established mentoring arrangements with charitable organizations.

Key learning points

▌ Best practice organizations ensure that there are a range of development activities that support talent management programmes.

▌ Developing a talent management programme is a cultural shift for some managers away from the 'referral' method of promotion.

My view is that a fair talent management *and* career management programme can make a significant difference for some organization's engagement scores. However, a word of caution: I have also seen several talent management schemes that have not succeeded, where the criteria were seen as unfair and where people on the programme were made empty promises of development and opportunities that did not emerge. A talent management programme needs to be well thought through and resourced in order for it to be effective.

To make your talent management programme a success:

▌ Invest time in defining what the future leadership needs of the organization are and in identifying talent.

▌ Do not be uncomfortable in discussing the issue of 'talent' openly. Employers with strong talent management practices and who communicate openly are perceived by their employees as having stronger and more effective leadership.

▌ Be prepared to over-invest in development. Hewitt research suggests that most companies invest 100–300 per cent more on high potentials than on the rest of their employee base.

▌ Encourage senior leaders to spend quality time with high performing people and to participate in some of the programmes.

REWARD AND RECOGNITION

Believing that you are fairly rewarded and recognized for the amount of work and effort that you put into a job is a key driver of engagement. A key question is: How much is financial reward the answer? Clearly base salary is important and compensation has always been in the top characteristics that are very important to job satisfaction. However, employees today look at the total work package.

In a recent study of UK companies with highly engaged staff, performance-related pay and recognition schemes were used more extensively than by the poorest performing organizations. Businesses with high levels of engagement were twice as likely as other UK organizations to use individual performance-related pay and various forms of individual and team recognition schemes, and five times as likely to use team or collective bonus schemes. A flexible benefits package is becoming more common and gives the individual freedom to make choices on how to divide up the rewards according to the priorities of that point in time.

Organizations need to give careful consideration to the range of reward and recognition that they offer their employees. My advice on rewards is to carry out a systematic and at least annual benchmark of remuneration to ensure that compared to your peer group's your policies are fair.

Equally important is the whole topic of recognition. The worst thing a manager can do is to ignore a direct report's effort or achievement.

Fewer than one in three employees in the United States can strongly agree that in the past seven days they have received recognition from their direct line manager, according to a Gallup survey. Yet we also know that people want to be recognized and appreciated.

One of the benefits of praise is that it releases a chemical in the brain called dopamine. This produces a 'feel-good factor' which in turn promotes positive emotions. The higher the level of positive emotions team members feel, the more engaged they are with the organization. However, waiting for the annual or bi-annual appraisal or the business 'star' awards ceremony is not enough. Employees who do not receive regular and genuine recognition are more likely to believe that nobody cares. According to research they are three times more likely to say that they will leave the organization in the next year. Conversely research by Gallup has shown that 'receiving recognition or praise for doing good work' can increase productivity and revenue by between 10 and 20 per cent.

So why don't managers give more praise? The brain is wired to notice the negative first. Certainly some managers I have worked with have stated that they do not need to praise or recognize someone who is working well as this is what they expected of the person in their job.

These managers tend in turn not to have managers who praise or recognize them. So it becomes a vicious circle: managers do not recognize their team members who in turn do not see the benefit of recognizing others.

Furthermore, my perception is that many managers believe that recognition needs to be linked to monetary reward. Although undoubtedly money is important, different people need different forms of recognition. Some may prefer a public pat on the back, others an accolade from their peers, others again may prefer a quiet word from their manager.

It is essential whatever the form the recognition takes that it should be sincere. In my opinion the problem with 'employee of the month' schemes is that people can perceive those people who receive recognition as not having truly deserved it. Managers were merely 'doing the rounds'.

However, as in the case of the optician retailer, where there was a marked absence of recognition, I do believe that some form of recognition scheme can 'kick start' a culture of more positive feedback.

Many organizations are now using recognition schemes as a means of acknowledging effort and achievement. Together with Steve Macaulay of Cranfield School of Management, I have devised some key questions for managers to ask when they devise a recognition scheme. These are:

▌ **Who** should be recognized – the company as a whole, groups or individuals?

▌ **Why** should they be recognized – eg for outstanding performance or improvement in customer service?

▌ **When** should this happen – on a one-off or on-going basis, eg as part of a regular reward scheme or performance management system?

▌ **What** form should the recognition take – eg financial or non-financial reward?

▌ **How** should the scheme be administered – eg what should be the method of delivering the reward or recognition?

The choice of approach needs to best fit the culture and climate of the organization. Nationwide Building Society has established an online recognition scheme. This allows the manager to select one of a range of rewards that they consider most appropriate to the individual (see more details in the case study later in this chapter). Vision Express fills its head office walls with letters of thanks and praise from its customers. At Claridges Hotel, any employee can be recognized by a peer, their manager or a guest. The individual receives a prize from a lucky dip. Prizes range from a stay at the hotel's luxury penthouse suite for a night through to time off and having a chauffer-driven limousine drive the individual home. In the United States at Stew Leonards an approach called MBA (Management By Appreciation) has been very successful. The walls of each outlet are full of photographs of employees of the month going back years.

Recognition, through token or monetary benefits, has got to be meaningful to those who receive it. Consistent with similar research undertaken by American Express, Air Miles found that its 1,000 employees (80 per cent of whom work in call centres) considered time off work the most significant form of reward. Air Miles implemented a recognition scheme called 'Time Off Vouchers' where individuals can be given time off in recognition of achievement.

Steve Macaulay and I have developed the following selection of eight practical exercises you can undertake to help develop a fair recognition scheme in your organization.

Survey your staff

It is surprising how many organizations assume they know best when it comes to recognition. Well-conducted surveys are a critical means to challenge assumptions.

First Direct believes it must continue to work at understanding its employees and the culture more deeply. It has introduced a Culture Critique, using staff focus groups, and one-to-one interviews not just with current employees but past ones too.

Train managers in why recognition is important

Managers have a key role to play in encouraging motivation among their team. Successful organizations provide training to managers in leadership and motivation. Julian Richer, of Richer Sounds, has considerable knowledge of building the right motivational climate. He believes managers should learn to follow five steps. These are:

▌ Make the workplace fun.

▌ Provide copious and specific recognition for the work that staff do.

▌ Offer frequent and targeted rewards.

▌ Make communication regular and all persuasive.

▌ Reward employee loyalty.

From scratch he has built up a thriving business worth in excess of £50 million on this basis and now offers advice in this area to other organizations such as Asda.

Give positive feedback

Reinforce in your managers the need to give positive feedback to their staff. A 'thank you' and 'well done' from the manager is often more meaningful to employees than a monetary or token award. FedEx rigorously champions managers as servicing their employees to service the customer.

Instigate a 'Job Well Done Award'

Sometimes immediate recognition of everyday good service can do a power of good. One car retailer runs a 'WOW' scheme where anyone in the organization can send a 'WOW' card to a member of staff who has gone out of their way to give them good service. At the end of each month, the number of cards is counted. Those people with the most cards win retail vouchers as a 'thank you'. Condant UK (formerly Credit Card Sentinel) runs 'Caught in the act' schemes where colleagues nominate others for awards, including spot prizes of Easter eggs, turkeys, teddy bears, T-shirts.

Feed back customer comments and compliments

Kwik-Fit keeps a customer correspondence folder in each depot reception area, publicizing positive letters customers have written. It rings up customers on a daily basis for feedback and publicizes the results internally.

Give departmental managers an allowance

Giving a sum of discretionary money, say £1,000 a year, to managers of teams to distribute in agreed ways can help promote a healthy, empowered environment. The team should be able to choose to distribute lots of small awards or fewer larger ones. Other ideas include non-monetary discretionary awards, such as retail vouchers and team T-shirts to record achievements. One manager of an IT service centre says 'A little thing like taking the trouble to buy ice-creams for everyone on a hot busy day lifts spirits; it's the thought that counts.'

Ensure that teams are recognized as well as individuals

Effective teamwork is at the heart of good service. At Whitbread Inns, an award scheme called 'Team Hospitality' was developed. The emphasis was on all members of the retail outlet working together to achieve success. Each outlet could obtain awards based on the team's performance. High-achieving outlets received a plaque to display in the customer-facing areas of their unit. This was highly prized. At Virgin, CEO Richard Branson throws regular parties as a 'thank you' for employees at his home.

Develop an award for good people management

FedEx's CEO Fredrick Smith comments 'When people are placed first, they will provide the highest possible service and profits will follow.' The company promotes good people management via an annual award. The award promotes positive role modelling, publicizing and promoting good practice in a very tangible form.

Nationwide case study

Building society Nationwide has moved from a paper-based to an online reward delivery system. Employing a large number of staff, the organization wanted to ensure that people understood their compensation package. The paper-based system it had was cumbersome and inefficient. Nationwide designed the new online programme called 'Fruitful' through consultation with employees. It developed a phased programme of introduction, starting by putting its 'Choices' programme online. This is a voluntary programme which includes benefits such as childcare vouchers, a home PC initiative and discounted goods and services. Nationwide found that the online system enabled it to better see who was taking up which benefits. This in turn allowed the organization to develop targeted communication campaigns to make employees aware of the benefits. The end result was the most successful scheme that the organization had run in terms of participation, with selections made by 50 per cent of employees covering 11,300 benefits options.

The online reward system now covers flexible benefits, rewards and recognition schemes, and compensation statements. These were launched on a rolling basis via a series of promotional teasers. In-branch training sessions heralded the changes. Particularly popular is the online recognition scheme where managers can e-mail a team member a non-cash recognition. The employee can then log onto their personal account to make a selection from a wide range of rewards from holidays to shopping vouchers.

Key learning points

▌ Ensure that you effectively communicate whatever scheme you use.

▌ Consider using an online reward scheme.

Checklist

Are the stages in your employees' journey fair?

How can you evidence this in terms of:

Recruitment and selection

Induction

Performance management

Learning and development

Talent management

Reward and recognition

Supporting HR policies – harassment, grievance and disciplinary procedures, retirement policies, etc.

Benchmark your organization against best practice.

This chapter has looked at the importance of fairness in relation to employee engagement. It has explained that fairness needs to run throughout the employee journey, starting with recruitment and selection through to the performance management process your business adopts and how people are rewarded and recognized. Fairness is the third aspect of the WIFI model. The fourth is involvement, which the next chapter addresses.

8

Involvement

The fourth aspect of the WIFI principle is involvement. Organizations with high levels of employee engagement recognize that communication is two way. They actively engage in conversation with their employees. Firms that involve their employees effectively are more likely to report high levels of employee engagement than firms that communicate less effectively. As we saw, information is an important factor in engagement. However, providing information on vision, values and goals alone will not engage staff. The counterpart of this top-down approach is a bottom-up one: involving staff means encouraging an open flow of two-way communication, empowering them to make decisions and giving them responsibility for their work. This is about listening to employees, asking for their feedback, seeking and acting on their ideas.

Many managers find providing information easier to do than involving employees in dialogue. Yet involvement is clearly a key feature of an engaged workforce. 'Ownership' is one of Spitzer's eight motivational desires, set out in Chapter 5. Involving people in decisions affecting their jobs helps increase psychological belonging and commitment.

This chapter looks at how leaders and managers in the business can engender high levels of involvement.

THREE LEVELS OF INVOLVEMENT

It makes sense that people who are involved and kept in the picture feel part of things and are able to do their jobs to the best of their ability. The opposite – a secretive climate, where people are kept in the dark, receiving little regular communication – makes people feel left out, vulnerable and exposed, which fuels an 'us and them' atmosphere of mistrust. As Jack Welch, CEO of GE said: 'Real communication is an attitude, it's an environment, it involves more listening than talking. It is a constant interactive process aimed at consensus.'

Creating a sense of involvement among employees needs to happen at three levels:

▌ with an employee's direct line manager;

▌ with other teams and groups;

▌ with the organization as a whole.

THE ROLE OF LINE MANAGERS

Employees involvement starts at a one-to-one level with their direct line manager. Have you ever worked for a manager who did not involve you in what was happening; who did not seek your ideas or act upon them; who did not allow you to make decisions relating to your work? I certainly have seen this in many locations. This quickly results in disillusionment and a reluctance to go the extra mile.

One example is a call centre environment in which I did some consulting. People worked in clusters or teams of 10–12 people. Typically people came in on a shift pattern. This started with a 'huddle' where people were told their targets for the day. It was a very sales-driven environment and highly monitored: people had to record when they went to the toilet and when they had a coffee break. Every hour each person's sales performance was recorded on a wall chart and people were measured on a daily and weekly basis on their performance. The rate of basic pay was low but consultants had the opportunity to increase their pay based on individual and team performance.

Individuals were supposed to have weekly coaching sessions with a sales coach but often these did not happen. Having listened to some of the sessions that did take place the emphasis was on what people were getting wrong and there was little praise.

Once a month there were half-hour team meetings where sales targets and performance figures were discussed. Information was cascaded about the business at these sessions but no opportunity was given for people to feed any ideas back. In essence information was flowing one way. Having attended one of these sessions I noticed that many people were sitting in their coats. I asked some of them why this was and it appeared that there were problems with heating in the building. Staff also complained that the coffee machine in their area had been broken for the past two weeks.

One of the reasons that I had been asked to visit the team was that attrition rates for the department were running at 40 per cent, compared to the industry average of 25 per cent. Customer complaints were rising and the management team were growing increasingly concerned that customers were saying they had been mis-sold.

It was immediately obvious that there were very low degrees of involvement and empowerment in the team. Speaking in turn to the team leaders and their managers it became apparent that they were not aware of the impact their management style was having on the team.

So why are managers reluctant to involve, delegate and empower their team members? The reason is primarily one of fear. This could include:

▌ fear of losing control if you allow people to come up with their own ideas;

▌ fear of losing your job if you delegate your tasks and they are done well;

▌ fear that the employee won't do the job to your required standards or in the time permitted;

▌ fear that the employee cannot be trusted to do the job unsupervised;

▌ fear of making a mistake in delegating and having to carry the responsibility for not completing the tasks.

Sometimes team members in turn may be afraid to get involved due to a lack of self-confidence, knowledge and training or just because they are 'afraid of the boss'.

To increase involvement scores signifies a breakthrough in managers' development because it implies recognition that others can help them do a better job than can be done alone, not only in terms of quantity and quality.

It often follows a crisis period when a backlog of unfinished work becomes an embarrassment or sales targets are not being met, or customer complaint levels are rising and managers realize that something must be done to stop things from grinding to a halt on certain fronts.

However, it is unusual for managers to want change the way that they work. If things are going badly it is easier to blame others rather than yourself. To give up duties that may have given them great satisfaction in first place is hard as is breaking the mindset that managers are the fountain of all knowledge. This is particularly the case where a manager has worked in a business that is very much his or her 'baby'. As the baby grows and develops it is no longer possible for them to do everything. The need to accept assistance becomes evident but the requirement to let go in certain areas is often resisted.

COACHING AND FACILITATION SKILLS

There are two key skills that managers need to help them create a more involving environment for their team members. These are coaching and facilitation skills.

Much has been written about coaching and I am a true believer in its power in creating ownership and responsibility in others. The issue with the call centre environment described above was the degree of dependency that individuals had on their managers. The environment had become one of parent–child with little opportunity for people to take responsibility for their own work or future development.

The first stage of turning the call centre environment around therefore was to improve the coaching skills of all the team leaders and managers. Coaching is a great tool for unlocking others' potential as it encourages them to take responsibility for their actions and personal development. Part of being able to coach effectively is the ability to provide balanced feedback. Developing the management team's feedback skills was also an important 'must'. We also ensured that the management team received coaching themselves around their personal development issues so that they could recognize its power.

Giving the management team training in coaching and feedback skills was the first step. The next was ensuring that they used a facilitative approach to the meetings and team interventions that they had. In particular, the training that we provided emphasized the need to ask questions to involve the group and to listen actively. We also covered team process techniques such as brainstorming and consensus generation.

A further step was to challenge managers' and team leaders' preconceptions about the extent which they could actually empower their teams. We worked through with them the empowerment model shown below, identifying areas where they could provide greater decision-making power to their team members. We also undertook a similar exercise with team members and then facilitated a discussion to compare the two results. This brought into the open issues around responsibility and trust, which the management team embraced.

The managers and team leaders started to apply their new skills. Gradually, as time progressed they became more involving and empowering with their team.

This manifested itself in a number of changes and initiatives:

▌ Team members were empowered to make customer decisions on the telephone without reference to team leaders.

▌ An improvement team was established to identify the reasons for this and to take action to resolve customer complaints.

▌ The agendas for team meetings were jointly agreed by team leaders and team members with the emphasis on two-way communication.

▌ Team meetings were chaired by members of the team on a rotational basis.

▌ Improvements were made as a result of staff suggestions to the working environment.

▌ Staff went on secondments to different parts of the business that they interacted with to improve their knowledge.

▌ Staff started working towards professional qualifications through the Institute of Customer Service.

▌ Improvement projects teams were established.

▌ Each team member was allied to a marketing product specialist so he or she became the ears and eyes of the customer for that particular product area.

▌ A social committee was established.

INVOLVEMENT WITH OTHER TEAMS

So coaching, feedback and facilitative skills are key building blocks for managers in involving their team members. On a more macro scale, involvement is also about feeling a sense of 'one team'. Engagement surveys undertaken by Hewitt Associates of 22 state-owned enterprises in China in 2004–05 found that one of the three top engagement factors along with work–life balance and work location was the relationship that employees have with their co-workers.

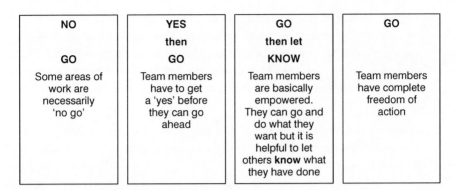

Figure 8.1 The empowerment model

A typical reaction when talking to people about teams other than their own is 'we work well together, it is the other teams that are the obstacles.' A natural reaction when you work in a team is to view other teams as competitors. Although this may be an instinctive response, it is not helpful. At times I have seen outward war between departments that has been far from healthy.

Many organizations put all their focus on developing effective work function teams and neglect the needs of cross-functional teamwork. Yet a lot of the frustrations of individual teams can be traced back to the departments who support them. These departments may well put up defensive barriers which hinder free-flowing processes. Important to engagement is the belief that employees can trust each other to do a good job, thus engendering a feeling of camaraderie and teamwork. Effective involvement across teams encourages greater levels of trust and customer focus. So what can managers do to encourage a spirit of 'one team'?

This was certainly an issue for the optician retailer, where people worked in isolated units and did not feel connected to the whole. There are various activities that organizations can undertake to actively encourage cross-functional involvement. These include the following:

▌ People can be encouraged to go and speak to others rather than using e-mail. For example, car manufacturer Honda has an open culture that encourages high levels of trust. Its people philosophy is based on the principle of its founder, Soichiro Honda: 'Yourself first, the company second.' The organization has developed a profile for the type of person that it wants to work in the company; it then trains employees in the skills and knowledge that they require to do their job well. Characteristics that it looks for in recruitment include plain speaking and optimism, interest and passion about the product. The organization promotes informal communication with a lot of cross-divisional contact. The underlying principle is to be proactive. New recruits are given a lot of autonomy and responsibility quickly which generates trust. The involvement of employees in decision making leads to a high degree of empowerment. This is deeply engrained in the culture rather than being a process.

▌ Secondments to other areas of the business and job swaps can be arranged. These can be very powerful in creating greater understanding between areas.

▌ Knowledge sharing groups can be established. Organizations then encourage representatives from different divisions to meet to share and identify best practice. One example is Royal Bank of Scotland, which has 40 brands across the group.

▌ Head office staff can be aligned to a customer-facing unit. For example, at sandwich chain Pret a Manger, head office managers are each allied to one of the chain's shops. They keep in touch with customers, employees and the brand by spending a day five times a year working in the outlet. The retailer encourages high levels of involvement with the chairman responding personally to all staff comments. All potential new recruits are given a day's 'Pret Experience' where the shop team are the final arbiters of whether they are taken on.

▌ Recognition of the internal customer is encouraged. Retailer Midlands Co-op conducts regular surveys of employees' satisfaction with the service they receive from each of its internal departments. The results of the survey are reviewed by the senior management team and improvement plans developed. The company has also changed the name of its head office to service centre in recognition of its function.

▌ Integrated teams can be created. For example, train operator GNER encourages team involvement at every level, delegating much responsibility. It has restructured its on-train crews to remove unnecessary barriers – catering staff are now part of an integrated cross-functional team, instead of being 'looked down upon'. This is reflected in staff turnover, which is down by a massive 66 per cent.

▌ An organization's rewards strategy can be based on teamwork: As a part of its change to integrated teams, GNER has adopted a team-based rewards strategy. It has found that this has greatly helped to generate a sense of one team.

▌ Teams can attending another area's team meetings. Simple as it sounds, this is a useful way of creating awareness of other teams' issues and generating better understanding and collaboration.

▌ Joint projects can be useful. Porsche in the United Kingdom formed a series of cross-functional project teams to tackle issues to improve customer service. The teams included representatives from the network franchise as well as head office functions. The results of the projects were not only improvements to external customer service but also greater understanding of the issues facing the dealerships.

▌ Another simple idea is to set up a 'getting to know you event – a 'trade fair' or series of stands, for example before or after town hall meetings, where each department has the opportunity to present who they are and what they do.

▌ Cross-functional training and development initiatives can be organized. When Pearl, the financial services organization, went through a rebranding exercise the key differentiators that employees saw for the brand were personal contact and individual service. The CEO decided that everyone should be involved in defining the brand for the future. With a workforce of 8,000 people, the executive decided to invest in a six-month event held every day for 50–60 people from a cross-section of functions in the organization. Each interactive day consisted of a series of exercises designed to involve employees in the brand and to generate their ideas for the future. Led each day by a member of the executive, the sessions were deemed a great success specifically because they encouraged cross-functional teamwork and sharing of ideas.

▌ Mentoring is another way of breaking down barriers. It can be particularly helpful for businesses with widespread geographic locations as it forces individuals to make contact with other parts of the group. Likewise, encouraging cross-functional promotion opportunities helps break down barriers.

▌ Fun days can be organized. Every year Hyundai Cars UK says thank you to the whole organization by holding a company team training day. Employees work in cross-functional teams to undertake activities linked to a development theme. The tone is light-hearted, participative and fun.

Key learning points

▌ Organizations can use a range of activities to break down cross-functional barriers and to create a sense of involvement.

The key is to actively promote activities that break down organizational silos.

INVOLVEMENT WITH SENIOR MANAGERS

A criticism that is often voiced by cynics, the actively disengaged people in the workforce, is that 'We have done it all before' and 'Managers just don't listen'. Sometimes, once you have climbed to the top of the ladder, you probably are more used to giving your opinion and making decisions than you are consulting and listening to others.

One of the issues that can cause senior managers to pay lip service to staff involvement is the very little time that they spend with staff experiencing life at the sharp end. Directors at DIY retailers B&Q, for example, found that even when they went 'back to the floor' for a day in a store, they were helped by the stores' employees and had very little direct contact with customers. (They overcame this on their next visit by vacating the store of its staff for the day so they truly had to go back to the floor.) Yet how many senior managers even spend one day a year in their outlets?

The first step of breaking down senior managers' reluctance to spending time devoted to staff involvement activities is to show them the benefits of involvement.

Case studies

National Australia Bank

At Australian financial services organization National Australia Bank, a cultural change programme established in the early 2000s has had lasting impact due in part to the power of bringing employees to senior managers. Used to having papers presented or Microsoft PowerPoint presentations made by managers to the senior executive committee, the bank broke the mould when it encouraged staff members who had taken part in the culture change programme to come in front of the executive to tell them exactly what the experience had meant for them. Employees were very natural. What they said was absolutely what they thought. It was such a stark difference from the sanitized material that the executives and board members were used to seeing that it got them really interested.

BUPA

When health care organization BUPA began a leadership development programme for team leaders and managers, the managing director of its insurance division decided to participate as a delegate in the programme. He worked in a group of six team leaders over the course of a four-day experiential learning event. This broke down barriers and misconceptions on both sides and allowed the managing director to understand team leader concerns better.

Key learning point

Find ways of bringing senior managers in direct contact with front-line staff. It helps increase better understanding of the issues staff face.

SENIOR MANAGERS AS ROLE MODELS

Simple as it sounds, one of the best ways of encouraging involvement in an organization is to ensure that senior managers are actively involved in leading involvement initiatives. Here are some examples that illustrate this principle.

General Motors case study

At General Motors a culture change programme was established in 2000 to bring about higher levels of employee engagement. Called 'Go Fast', the programme was based on GE's 'Work Out' model. The concept was to get cross-organization, cross-discipline and cross-hierarchy groups involved in identifying blockages to productivity and customer focus and empowering them to overcome these. Senior managers have been actively involved in the process by sponsoring at least two 'Go Fast' sessions each year. As the CEO and his direct staff tend to make evidence-based decisions, the key to engaging them in the process was to provide facts around the importance and potential impact of their involvement.

Once commitment was obtained, GM trained its leaders to organize and facilitate the 'Go Fast' sessions. In addition, each department trained at least one person to be a 'Go Fast' coach. A process was established whereby when any employee identified a problem that affected his or her work the employee contacted a facilitator who would speedily arrange a 'Go Fast' session. These typically lasted two days, involved around 12 people who had knowledge or experience of the problem and were sponsored by one of the senior management team. Participants would identify the components of the problem and brainstorm potential solutions, they would analyse each option and then make recommendations for improvement. These were put to the sponsor and an agreed decision-making panel who ratified the recommendations and assigned responsibilities for their implementation.

The reason that the 'Go Fast' sessions were so successful and have now become part of the General Motors culture is that senior managers' responsibility for holding a minimum of two sessions a year was built into their yearly objectives. Senior managers were keen to demonstrate to their peers that they were actively taking part in the initiative and the value of the session outputs.

Case studies

MBNA

Some time ago MBNA, the credit card company, discovered that it took five years on average to recoup the investment required to attract new customers. Yet the typical customer tenure was only four years. The CEO enlisted the aid of employees to help him find the root cause of why customers were leaving. Members of staff interviewed customers who had recently changed to another supplier. They uncovered a wealth of complaints from customers that had caused them to switch cards. The CEO then set up working parties to come up with ways to address these issues, boosting satisfaction and retention. At the same time the very act of asking employees to find solutions boosted the levels of engagement.

AA Business Services

As part of a change effort called Osprey, AA Business Services set out to improve its communications considerably. The Osprey programme was a success in raising very low staff morale that was a result of redundancies and poor business performance, and in making a quantum improvement in service performance. Senior managers led the way to consciously model the more open communication required in the new organization. At all stages in the design and implementation of changes, staff were encouraged to comment, and express their opinions and concerns.

Managers spread the word on strategy and company issues and channelled difficulties or blockages to working groups of senior management for resolution. The key company message was that positive, well-trained staff would attract new customers and retain existing ones by being 'the trusted first choice for customers'.

It was felt that communication would improve as a result of managers being more skilled in the principles and practices of communication. Skills development in these areas was introduced as part of a wider development programme. These skills were then developed in groups of staff at all levels, emphasizing the message that business understanding was everyone's responsibility, not just the responsibility of managers or the HR department. The results demonstrated improvement: productivity up 16 per cent in the first year, 18 per cent in the next, with lower costs and substantial service performance improvement. It was recognized that considerable effort and resources had been deployed on the people issues as the change process stepped up.

Reuters

In 2003 when Reuters began a three-year transformation plan to stop itself going under, the CEO sponsored an online database to allow anyone in the company from across the world to register an issue. The only caveat was that for each issue raised a solution had to be put forward. The website was open for two weeks and received 2,000 responses. Within three days of the website's closure all members of the senior management team had a copy of the issues raised. The ideas were categorized on the intranet under the title of the CEO's challenges. Teams of Reuters staff were then actively engaged in tackling the issues raised and making the solutions work. In the annual engagement survey that followed there was an overwhelmingly increased score for the level of engagement.

Key learning points

▌ When senior managers become directly and actively involved in the listening process and empower employees to act on recommendations, engagement levels rise.

▌ It can be useful to hold senior managers accountable for employee involvement activities by building this into their objectives.

▌ Providing training to managers in communication skills and facilitation techniques can help improve their ability to involve others.

INTERNAL COMMUNICATIONS DEPARTMENTS

Effective involvement does not happen without determined effort and perseverance. To ensure that everyone understands and acts on customer and employee needs, communication needs to be open, two-way and frequent. Once staff become more involved in the work environment and believe that they are listened to they are more willing to come up with ideas. Nissan UK suggests that 90 per cent of changes to its current production comes from people doing the job.

As mentioned in Chapter 6, leaders have a large part to play in encouraging a one-team approach. As the head of internal communications for a major blue-chip corporation recently commented 'a decade ago the "internal communications department" was an ex-journalist who churned out the employee newsletter once a month'. Now in best practice organizations internal communications is an important corporate function, the principal tasks of which focus on employee engagement. My belief is that internal communications should be part of the HR function because what it does is provide a conduit for employee engagement strategies to come to life.

Checklist

What does your company do in terms of involvement?

Use this checklist to rate your own organization's track record in terms of involvement.

	In place and effective	In place but could be improved	Not in place but needs to be
1. Your own team			
Team members have regular contact with everyone in the team including people whose jobs are remote			
Your team leader asks for and acts on team members' suggestions			
Your team holds periodic improvement events to stimulate new ideas			
Your teams makes best use of all available communications methods, eg face-to-face meetings, e-mail, newsletters, videoconferencing, intranet, internet			
2. Cross-team working			
There are opportunities available for teams to work with other teams			
Teams are encouraged to work collaboratively with other teams			
3. Senior leaders...			
Actively sponsor and encourage employee involvement			
Ask for and act on new ideas			

This chapter has looked at the fourth aspect of the WIFI principle, involvement. It has examined the following principles. Organizations with high levels of employee engagement recognize that communication is two-way. They actively engage in conversation with their employees. Firms that involve their employees effectively are more likely to report high levels of employee engagement than firms that communicate less effectively.

The subsequent chapters address the role of the HR professional, leaders and managers in driving and sustaining changes in levels of employee engagement.

9

Agents for change

Having outlined the elements of the WIFI model that lead to high levels of employee engagement, this chapter provides advice for those responsible for making this happen:

▌ HR professionals and change agents;

▌ leaders;

▌ managers.

Undoubtedly, HR can play a key role as an agent for change and in promoting employee engagement. If you are reading this book you would presumably like to affect change in your organization. This chapter looks at the role of the HR professional, consultant or manager who wants to act as an agent for change in their organization and how they can achieve this.

In addition, having gained buy-in to an employee engagement strategy that identifies each of the key drivers for WIFI, this chapter outlines the importance of the active support of the leadership team in acting as role models for employee engagement. It also summarizes the leadership practices that help create an engaged workforce.

EMPLOYEE CHAMPIONS

HR professionals have a unique role to play in championing employee engagement and its benefits to the business. However, HR's ability to do this is limited to the sphere of influence that they have. Too often they are seen as a 'support service' and not business focused or strategic. Typically, most managers would say that that people are vital to the future of their organizations, yet only a small minority believe HR currently plays a crucial role in strategy formulation and operational results.

One of the reasons that the HR director of the optician retailer was able to develop and start delivering on an employee engagement strategy was that she was aware of who to bring on board early in the process and how to get the CEO to act as sponsor and give their active support.

Conversely, I have worked with HR professionals who have been aware of what needs to change but have not had the ability to influence others to do this. The sustainable success of an employee engagement strategy is often dependent on how well senior HR managers and HR business partners develop relationships with their key stakeholders.

There are four key skills that change agents and HR professionals need to develop to be successful in this arena:

▌ ability to read the political landscape;

▌ influencing skills;

▌ coaching skills;

▌ marketing skills.

ABILITY TO READ THE POLITICAL LANDSCAPE

If you are embarking on an employee engagement strategy or you wish to enhance one you already have, one of the first steps is to become more aware of the political context of your organization. Every organization is political and as an HR professional and change agent it is essential that you are able to read the political situation. When implementing change, consider:

▌ Who will be a winner?

▌ Who will be a loser?

▌ Who can help drive change?

▌ Who will hinder change?

When you identify people who will lose out because of the change and who may hinder progress, consider how you can get them on board. What concerns do you need to address to help them see the benefits of change? How can you actively involve them in a solution?

INFLUENCING SKILLS

Part of the skill set of the effective change manager is to be able to influence effectively. There are two main styles of influence: one is push, the other is pull.

Push is a 'tell' style where the HR professional and/or change agent states views and opinions, offers incentives and consequences and states expectations. The impact on the other person is to signal that the speaker wishes the other person to change.

The pull style of influence is focused much more on asking questions, listening and building common ground. The impact of this style is one of signalling willingness to change.

To influence effectively the change manager needs to know when to use a push style of influence and when to use a pull.

COACHING SKILLS

Once you have established a sponsor for your programme and gained buy-in for engagement, a further role the HR professional should hold is that of coach.

Engagement programmes go quickly off the track if what senior managers say and do is incongruent with the principles of well-being, information, fairness and involvement.

If you sit at the top table or are an HR business partner, you have a powerful role to take in providing feedback and coaching to the team on what they could do more of or do differently to encourage engagement. Part of your role should be to act as the conscience of your senior leadership or team. Typically, senior leaders receive little direct feedback on their behaviours and the impact that these have on others.

If it is not appropriate for you to act as coach yourself, it may be a good idea to encourage managers to use the services of an external coach or mentor. One chief executive I know has three external coaches. They are each helping him to work on aspects of their personal and business development. Having coaching at a senior level (and not being afraid to say you are) and/or acting as a mentor for other people in the business sends positive messages to the rest of the organization about the power of ongoing development.

MARKETING SKILLS

A further set of skills that you should develop as an HR professional or change agent relate to how to market the programme to employees. For too long marketing and HR have sat as separate disciplines reporting to different people at board level. Part of the success of employee engagement activities is being able to market these positively to employees so that they are aware of their existence.

One company I know, for example, identified via its employee engagement survey that there were two key areas for improvement. The company made major efforts to increase its training and development portfolio and to offer a better benefits scheme. An e-mail was sent to all staff telling them about the changes and management waited for the response. As you would expect, people were slow to respond and there was little take up of the new options.

If you do not have the internal marketing skills, you should consider employing or seconding an internal marketer on to your team. Internal marketing or internal communications personnel should report directly to HR and be part of that department.

If you are developing an overall employee engagement strategy it is suggested that you develop four work streams to address well-being, information, fairness and involvement, and that you then have another one that is about internal marketing. If you consider your employees as your customers, internal marketing is important to attract and retain loyalty to your brand.

THE KEY ROLE OF LEADERS

I cannot stress enough how important your business leaders are to driving the employee engagement agenda. The worst thing that can happen to your programme is to get sign off and then for the executive to leave it to you to drive the strategy and make engagement happen.

An important aspect of employee engagement is how employees feel about the head of the company and senior managers – the degree to which employees trust their leaders and believe they are accessible.

LEADERSHIP PRACTICES

The style of leadership that is demonstrated by senior managers at the top of the organization in turn influences the behaviours of managers throughout the organization. If a CEO's style of leadership is controlling and closed, the probability is that the organizational culture will not be empowering or innovative and in turn employees are unlikely to connect to the organization emotionally. Leadership is also the driver of the organization's vision, strategy and values. These in turn influence policies and processes as well as management behaviour, communication and teamwork.

Employee engagement only develops with top–down commitment and constant follow-through by senior managers. The starting point for engagement therefore is to ensure that the senior management team not only believe in the importance of engagement but also actively role model the behaviours that promote engagement.

The issue is that as managers climb the organizational ladder, they start to hit problems they had not encountered before. They become increasingly visible and vulnerable – people watch and read what they do and their impact is greater. They also have external draws such as shareholders and key stakeholders which can mean that they need to focus on managing external relationships. It is easy therefore for leaders to become less accessible to employees and to spend a large percentage of their time engrossed in external affairs.

Senior managers can make a real difference to people's working lives and performance, yet many have issues around visibility, communications and employee involvement. Part of the role of the change agent is to have the courage to address these issues in a positive and proactive manner.

BUILDING EMPLOYEE ENGAGEMENT

The principles of WIFI (well-being, information, fairness and involvement) apply to leaders in the organization as much as managers. Critical actions senior leaders can take to build employee engagement are:

▌ communicating a clear vision of the future;

▌ building trust in the organization;

▌ involving employees in decision making that will affect them;

▌ demonstrating commitment to the company values;

▌ being seen to respond to feedback.

Sun Microsystems case study

Hemant Sharma, Head, HR, Sun Microsystems India, explained in an article on the Vertex website how his organization has successfully managed to engage its virtual workforce through the active involvement of senior managers in the programme:

Employee engagement is imperative for an organization like Sun as we operate in virtual teams across the globe. Employee engagement becomes that much more critical in such a virtual environment.

At Sun, we treat our employees with utmost importance. The concept of employee engagement starts right from the top with Scott McNealy our CEO and the senior management team. Scott interacts with our employees through WSUN, a forum on Sun's intranet where he engages in active dialogue once a month on corporate goals and directions, and also solicits [employees'] feedback, opinions and pet peeves.

[Another] senior management member... Jonathan Schwartz, COO, engages with employees on technology directions through his personal blog. Our business unit Heads and Executive Vice-presidents have a target of holding six 'town halls' with employees every year across the globe.

At the country level in India, senior management is constantly engaging employees through various forums and interactions to build excitement and passion through various communication channels and events. In fact, we also reach out to the employees' families by inviting and involving them in some events.

The internal website of Sun is updated daily, thus keeping employees abreast of the happenings and developments in their organization.

PROVIDING ONGOING DEVELOPMENT FOR LEADERS

How do your leaders rate on the qualities listed above the case study? My guess is that there will be a range of skills and attributes in your leadership population. As discussed earlier, part of the change agent's role is to encourage and facilitate ongoing learning and development for the leadership team.

One model to use at a senior level to help identify the development needs of senior managers is the model of the intelligences. To be successful at a senior level, leaders require a set of skills, behaviours and knowledge that relate to four intellects: business intelligence (BQ), political intelligence (PQ), spiritual intelligence (SQ) and emotional intelligence (EQ).

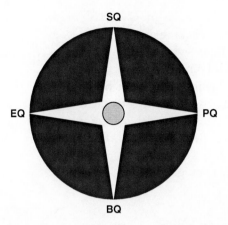

Figure 9.1 The compass of the intellects

Depicted as four points of a compass (as in Figure 9.1), these intellects help leaders to navigate the business landscape. Like the four points of a compass, they have equal weight. If the leader is missing one or more of the intellects, the compass becomes imbalanced and unreliable, the pathway unclear.

BQ involves:

▌ business expertise or competence;

▌ thinking ahead strategically;

▌ listening to and anticipating customer demands;

▌ planning to meet customer demands;

▌ developing customer-driven offerings and solutions;

▌ taking opportunities to improve services to the customer.

Leaders with BQ anticipate changing customer demands. They translate this knowledge into service offers and operational processes that deliver successfully to the customer. They are proactive in managing customer expectations and ensure that their businesses are customer friendly.

Stelios Haji Ioannou typifies someone with high BQ. When he established his business, easyJet, he aimed to provide a low-cost, no-frills style airline which anticipated a growing trend towards inexpensive travel. His model has challenged and changed the face of European travel. It has been extended into other areas such as car rental and the internet where he has stripped out complicated and expensive business procedures. Although it is early days in the application to a wide range of sectors, he has made it easy for customers to do business with his organization while still opening up the possibility of making money.

Leaders with high levels of BQ will often have strengths in the inform element of the WIFI model.

Emotions and feelings play a much bigger role in business than is sometimes recognized in a rationally orientated management world. The ability to recognize your own and others' emotions and the impact that these emotions have is critical. Behaviours that demonstrate EQ include:

- understanding feelings of self and others;
- listening;
- being open and empathic;
- sharing feelings;
- appreciating others.

EQ can have a direct financial impact. For example, when researchers in the United States studied the emotional intelligence of GPs, they discovered that those with lowest level of empathy were more likely to have been sued by their patients.

EQ relates to the quality of relationships between managers, their bosses, colleagues and direct reports. A study of leaders who took part in the BT global challenge Round the World Yacht Race in 2001 showed that the more successful boats tended to have skippers and crews with higher levels of EQ than those who were unsuccessful in the race.

Leaders with high levels of EQ will often have strengths in the fairness and involvement elements of the WIFI model.

The term 'spiritual intelligence', or SQ, was promoted by Zohar and Marshall, who observed that in these rapidly changing times it was important to have a personal anchor. They described this as one's values and contribution, combined with a willingness to be receptive to new ideas and information.

Leaders with SQ display a high degree of self-confidence and self-awareness that enables them to set a clear direction and to stick firm to their course of action while not shutting out important new pieces of information. They have thought through well:

- their life and purpose;
- their role goals and contribution;
- their value to 'the world';

▌ how they can personally grow and develop self-awareness.

This spirituality provides inner strength and helps form a personal vision. Leaders with high SQ can be very inspirational to others. Leaders such as Nelson Mandela and author Stephen Covey display SQ through a clear set of personal values and beliefs that drive their actions. In times of change a clear sense of identity and self-belief are essential. People with strong SQ have the personal resources to drive the formulation of strong and appealing organizational visions and values. They exert a strong influence that drives the behaviours of others towards future goals. Their strength of conviction gives them the confidence to think outside the box and not to be afraid to do things differently.

Leaders with high levels of SQ will often have strengths in the well-being element of the WIFI model.

Leaders need to be aware of how to influence others in the organization. Every organization is political but the word also carries other negative connotations such as self-seeking manipulation that lead managers to shy away from its existence. PQ as we define it involves:

▌ being aware of power bases;

▌ understanding sources of power;

▌ recognizing levers of influence during change;

▌ developing strategies for influence;

▌ gaining buy-in from stakeholders.

Leaders with high levels of PQ will often have strengths in the involvement element of the WIFI model.

The compass model of these four sets of behaviours can work well as a discussion starter on the development needs of your leadership team.

HELPING LEADERS IDENTIFY THEIR DEVELOPMENT NEEDS

The plain fact is that senior managers often have high BQ and their PQ may be enhanced, but they display low EQ and SQ levels so they fail to connect with their employees. Often poor at communicating, leaders fail to engender trust in their employees. Trusting what the leaders in the business say is one of the key drivers of employee engagement.

In the United States, the organization Great Place to Work conducts an annual survey on behalf of *Fortune* magazine to identify the top 100 places to work in the United States. It has developed a 'Trust Index' as a measure of employee engagement. Companies that connect well with their employees in the study include the following.

Federal Express, which has 120,000 employees, always features high in the Trust Index. The company has an incredibly low 'voluntary' staff turnover of 4 per cent. The company pays well and has never had to lay staff off. Federal Express has its own television station so that the CEO can talk to all of the employees worldwide. He will also answer unprompted questions live. Of the company's 18 senior vice presidents, 16 started in the company in non-management jobs. So everyone knows and trusts them – and there is a strong belief in promotion from within.

In US retail environments, the turnover is always high. Nordstrom is always in the Trust Index top 100, but has the highest staff turnover of these 100 companies at 43 per cent. However, 3,000 of the organization's 35,000 employees have worked for Nordstrom for over 10 years. All of Nordstrom's senior people started in the stock room or on the selling floor, so they understand how employees wish to be treated. For example, they close all the stores on New Year's Day and also the Fourth of July (Independence Day) so that staff can spend time with their families.

ENGENDERING TRUST

Although business journals are brim full of articles about leadership, there are some simple maxims that leaders can follow to create and engender trust. They should:

- have a clear vision of where they want the organization to be;
- clearly and persuasively communicate this vision to employees;
- involve employees in how to achieve the vision;
- align their own behaviours to the behaviours needed to achieve the vision and be consistent in demonstrating these.

Essentially this boils down to four sets of behaviours, as shown in Figure 9.2.

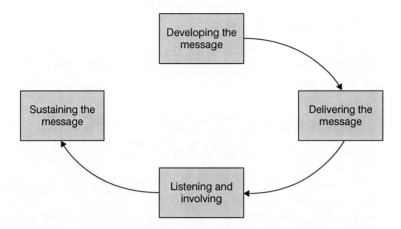

Figure 9.2 Four sets of behaviours

Tesco case study

Retailer Tesco provides a good example of these leadership principles. As one of the United Kingdom's biggest businesses, it has gone from competing in the East End to competing on a world stage. How has it achieved this?

Tesco's CEO Terry Leahy stated publicly at the Institute of Directors Annual Conference in London in 2006:

> There are four main things that have really made a difference to our ability to compete internationally. The first is that we have been clear about what we wanted to achieve. The second is that we have listened to what our customers have told us. The third is that we have given responsibility to our managers and staff. The fourth is that we have tried to keep things simple. These principles apply to businesses of any size.
>
> Shortly after I took over Tesco, we sat down with thousands of our staff and asked ourselves some simple questions: what was the business for, what did we believe in, where did we want to go as a company? This is what we came up with. Our core purpose was expressed in one short sentence: to create benefit for customers, to earn their lifetime loyalty. Our values – just two: try harder than anyone else for your customers; treat people how you would like to be treated. Our strategy – just four things: build a strong core business in the UK; become as strong in non-food as we were in food; develop a profitable retailing services business; be as strong internationally as were domestically.

Key learning point

Senior leaders can build strong companies by listening and involving staff.

COMMUNICATE, COMMUNICATE, COMMUNICATE

Part of your role as a change agent should be to help leaders to improve their ability to inform and involve.

A major study by Watson Wyatt, *Connecting Organizational Communication to Financial Performance*, found that 'a significant improvement in communication effectiveness is associated with a 29.5 per cent increase in market value' and that 'companies with the highest levels of effective communication experienced a 26 per cent total return to shareholders from 1998 to 2002, compared to a 15 per cent return experienced by firms that communicate least effectively'.

Most leaders focus on 'hard' measures, delivering the required organizational outcomes on time, on budget and on target. Communication is often seen as a 'bolt on', yet it is the biggest driver of organizational performance leaders have at their disposal.

The strength of leaders often lies in 'delivering the message', presenting at conferences and events about the performance of the business. What is not often a strength is the degree to which leaders listen and involve their employees. This, by its very nature, has to be more of a one-to-one event rather than a one-to-group event.

Leaders at Wegmans Food Markets, for example, who were number 1 in 2005 on the *Fortune* top 100 list, set up a series of informal store visits to ensure that Wegman's most senior executives and employees are on a first name basis. As one employee explained to *Fortune* magazine:

> Communication from upper level management, including our CEO, to all employees makes this place great. I do appreciate the messages left on voicemail when important announcements are made. Also, I appreciate his calls thanking us for our hard work. He knows it takes all of us to make this company successful and I appreciate that.

A critical element in building trust is encouraging leaders to ask questions of employees from the perspective of not knowing all the answers, but seeking suggestions, listening actively and acting on ideas. If the leader is open to ideas, there is an opportunity to open up a deeper level of communication.

When Greg Dyke was running the BBC he began a series of forums to encourage employees to embrace change and think what might be. He personally attended the events, listened and endorsed the findings. When he was asked to leave the corporation, employees showed their commitment to his approach by going on strike.

Key learning points

▌ Trust is engendered when leaders are seen as approachable and accessible.

▌ It is important that leaders listen, consult and involve employees and act on their ideas.

▌ The problem with many 'communication events' that leaders attend is that the dialogue is often one way. Yet, as we have seen, involvement is equally as important as information giving.

DEVELOPING LISTENING SKILLS

Many leaders have not developed their communication skills, particularly in terms of listening, and inviting and acting on feedback and ideas. They may have reached their positions based on BQ and know-how but not know how to put people at their ease, really to listen and to relate to others. Research outlined by Goleman (1996) demonstrates that up to 80 per cent of the success of an effective leader is down to their EQ.

Ex-Communications Director of Fedex, Ed Robertson, identified 11 interpersonal skills that characterized effective leadership communication. These are:

▌ active listening;

▌ empathetic listening;

▌ checking accuracy;

▌ clarifying meaning;

▌ disclosing emotion;

▌ encouraging input;

▌ providing feedback;

▌ soliciting feedback;

▌ giving instructions;

▌ managing conflict;

▌ managing constructive feedback.

You will notice that most of these skills relate to involvement rather than information giving. So how do you convince senior leaders of the need to personally develop these skills?

Here are a couple of techniques that have proved useful in my consulting experience: personal reflection and using 180- or 360-degree feedback to identify strengths and development needs.

PERSONAL REFLECTION

Most leaders buy in intellectually to the notion that they need to promote well-being, inform, promote fairness and involve. However, ask them to reflect on their personal actions in these areas and you may start a meaningful dialogue about where they need to change. Below are some questions that you could discuss individually with members of the senior leadership team to see how well they currently role model leadership engagement activity.

USING FEEDBACK

Another area that also helps identify strengths and development areas for senior leaders is the use of 180-degree (if the person is the CEO) and 360-degree feedback. I used it, for example, with the leadership group of the optical retailer and used the results to develop personal coaching plans.

360-degree feedback is a useful tool to raise leaders' awareness of the emotional and spiritual aspects of their leadership style that they may need to develop. We worked with one CEO who asked for feedback from the chairman, colleagues and employees across the business to see how he could better communicate and whether his behaviours were consistent with the values that the organization was espousing.

At telecommunications corporation BT, 360-degree appraisal is compulsory for all top managers. It has found it has promoted:

▌ greater and more explicit understanding of customer needs;

▌ specific targets for employee engagement which can be measured;

▌ mutual cooperation between supplier and customer.

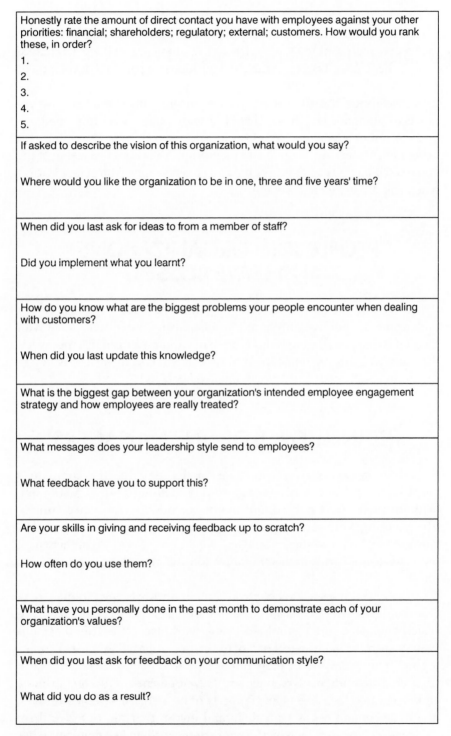

Honestly rate the amount of direct contact you have with employees against your other priorities: financial; shareholders; regulatory; external; customers. How would you rank these, in order?

1.

2.

3.

4.

5.

If asked to describe the vision of this organization, what would you say?

Where would you like the organization to be in one, three and five years' time?

When did you last ask for ideas to from a member of staff?

Did you implement what you learnt?

How do you know what are the biggest problems your people encounter when dealing with customers?

When did you last update this knowledge?

What is the biggest gap between your organization's intended employee engagement strategy and how employees are really treated?

What messages does your leadership style send to employees?

What feedback have you to support this?

Are your skills in giving and receiving feedback up to scratch?

How often do you use them?

What have you personally done in the past month to demonstrate each of your organization's values?

When did you last ask for feedback on your communication style?

What did you do as a result?

Figure 9.3 Questions for senior leaders

Fedex is an example of another organization that has upward appraisal as part of its culture to set training and development targets for its top managers. Every employee completes a questionnaire on the performance of his or her leader. The results help the creation of a personal development plan.

As leaders are always pressed for time, encouraging learning at work in practical situations is a must. There is a wide range of learning methods open to senior managers, in addition to classroom-based training, and development such as coaching and mentoring. You should be aware of the options so that you can have meaningful conversations with senior leaders when you discuss their development.

PEOPLE JOIN ORGANIZATIONS AND LEAVE BOSSES

If you wish to increase levels of engagement in your business, do not underestimate the pivotal role of the relationship individuals have with their line manager. Although this is often not acknowledged by employees, the quality of this relationship employees have with their boss is key in promoting high levels of employee engagement.

THE INFLUENCE OF LINE MANAGERS

Front-line managers are responsible for the majority of a company's employees and most of its day-to-day dealings with customers. Without their effort and commitment, business performance suffers. The BlessingWhite study on engagement, for example, shows that employees who know their managers 'well' or 'very well' trust them a lot more, have more pride in their organization and are willing to go the extra mile.

Although employees do not always admit openly to this, studies show that their direct line manager has an enormous impact on the degree to which employees are committed to the workplace. It is true that individuals are more likely to feel part of the organization if they trust and have a good relationship with their immediate line manager. Yet in a 2006 Chartered Institute of Personnel and Development survey one in three employees said their line manager rarely or never discussed their training and development needs with them and one in four did not give them feedback on how they were performing, or make them feel that their work counted. A further US survey found that only one-tenth would turn to their immediate boss for workplace advice. In contrast, one quarter of respondents would turn to a colleague in their organization for help and around one in six to another senior person at work, a friend outside work or a mentor or coach.

So why is it that, in surveys such as these, employees score their bosses so low? Many organizations do not offer sufficient management development opportunities for their employees. One key action that you could take if you want to improve engagement scores is to offer more development to your managers.

Furthermore, the level of employee engagement is not a criterion used in the measurement of managers' performance in many organizations. Few managers are aware of the key actions that research indicates they can take to raise their employee engagement scores.

Steps managers can take to increase engagement

Here is a list of the key actions that research indicates managers can take to engage their teams:

- Be clear about what is expected of each person in their role.

- Value individual contributions.

- Care for the individual as a person.

- Trust the individual.

- Involve individuals in decision making.

- Encourage the expression of opinions, listen and act on these.

- Provide regular motivational and developmental feedback.

- Recognize a job well done.

- Review individual performance on a one-to-one basis at least once every six months.

AXA case study

Asia-Pacific financial services organization AXA employs over 4,000 people in Australia, New Zealand, Hong Kong, China, Singapore, the Philippines, Indonesia, Thailand, India and Malaysia. The organization has developed an employee engagement programme linked to their customer proposition to 'Be life confident'.

Being 'life confident' is about reassuring people that they can progress and grow. AXA's goal is to provide a work environment that enables AXA people to 'be life confident'. Its employee engagement programme can help them to:

▌ be connected, by establishing the link to individual values and person-alizing the experience;

▌ be challenged, by raising the bar, being open to new experiences and seeing things in different ways;

▌ be giving, by having a truly generous spirit that gives without exception;

▌ be balanced, by finding ways to integrate work and life – it's not about 'either/or', it's about 'and';

▌ be recognized, by acknowledging and rewarding and in turn increasing the level of engagement.

AXA places a lot of emphasis on leadership and talent management. This is underpinned by a leadership competency framework, which is incorp-orated into individual performance objectives for all leadership positions. Good communication is promoted via a number of vehicles: *AXA Tracks*, a monthly magazine for Australian and New Zealand businesses, and regular updates on the intranet, provide employees with information on how the business has been performing, new developments, AXA community activities and other articles of interest.

Senior leaders and managers' active involvement in the programme is seen as key to its success. Every year the Global AXA Group conducts 'SCOPE', a worldwide employee engagement survey. Over 4,300 AXA Asia Pacific employees, and 67,000 employees in the Global AXA Group completed the survey in 2006. The results for Asia-Pacific put the organi-zation in the top quartile of engagement scores.

SUPPORT AND CHALLENGE

One of the key actions that you should take as an agent for change is to find ways (eg through development opportunities, performance reviews, measurement systems) to emphasize that managers need to demonstrate two sets of behaviours: both support and challenge.

Supportive behaviours include:

▌ offering motivational feedback;

▌ listening;

▌ empathizing;

▌ providing assistance, guidance and backup for others;

▌ helping with resources or giving their own time and effort.

Challenging behaviours are:

▌ offering developmental feedback;

▌ challenging others to do better by making requests and setting targets;

▌ asking others to rethink their actions and decisions by questioning and offering alternatives;

▌ confronting issues assertively.

When a manager uses a highly challenging but low supporting style the environment created is often stressful and task focused. A manager who uses high support but low challenge creates a 'cosy' environment, where the emphasis is on maintaining relationships but not necessarily getting things done. An environment of low challenge and low support can lead to apathy and low morale. A manager who uses a high challenge style but also high support is most likely to create a motivating, high-performance culture.

You can assess your own preferences for supportive and challenging behaviour by undertaking the assessment at the end of this chapter.

THE LINK TO FEEDBACK

Feedback can help a manager maintain and improve their team members' performance and play an important part in creating employee engagement and a high-performance culture.

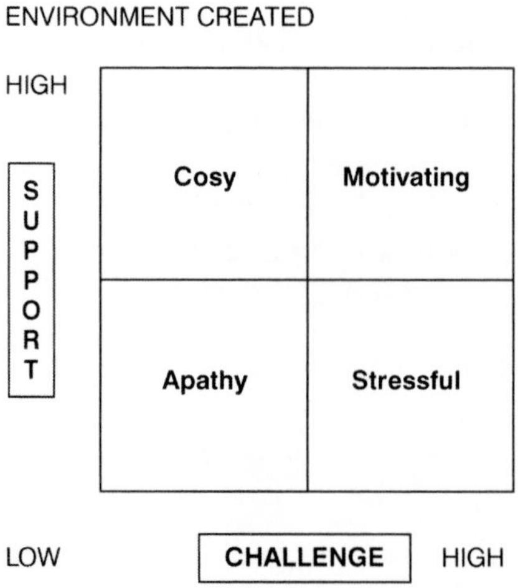

ENVIRONMENT CREATED

HIGH

	Cosy	Motivating
S U P P O R T	Apathy	Stressful

LOW   **CHALLENGE**   HIGH

Figure 9.4   Support and challenge

If your scores indicate that you create a 'cosy' environment (high support and low challenge), it is likely that you will be comfortable giving motivational feedback to others (feedback on what has gone well) but not so happy giving developmental feedback (feedback on where the individual can improve). If you create a stressful environment you will readily give developmental feedback but not so readily give praise or recognition. If your scores are in the apathy box it is likely that you do not give much feedback at all. Where the ideal score should be is in the motivating environment where you are likely to give balance motivational and development feedback.

As the purpose of feedback is to improve performance and to keep people on track, providing feedback on performance should be a regular part of a manager's role. So why do many managers neglect this important activity or leave it to the once-yearly performance review? Here are some of the possible reasons.

Some people hold back from giving motivational feedback for the following reasons:

▌ They think that compliments are inappropriate, because staff are only doing what they are paid to do.

▌ They feel too embarrassed.

▌ They believe that the person receiving the feedback may relax and take it easy.

▌ They believe that the person receiving the feedback may be suspicious of their motives.

▌ They think that the feedback may be misinterpreted as a ploy to fish for compliments in return.

▌ They don't like receiving motivational feedback themselves.

Some people hold back from giving developmental feedback for these reasons:

▌ They worry that they might upset the receiver.

▌ They are concerned that the receiver may reject them or reject the feedback.

▌ They are concerned that the person might retaliate with developmental feedback themselves.

▌ They are concerned that it may end in a confrontation that would be difficult to resolve and might damage future relations.

▌ They think that the issue is too trivial, and that the feedback would be better saved up for something more substantial.

▌ They don't like receiving developmental feedback themselves.

However, if managers do not provide regular feedback it is easy for employees to become de-motivated and go off track. Employees are left with a feeling of not being valued, trusted and cared for as a person or involved in decision making. They may not be clear about the expectations of them in their role or feel that their job or contribution is important.

BELIEFS ABOUT FEEDBACK

Fundamental to being able to give effective feedback is the belief that feedback is a helpful, healthy and positive communication between two people. The purpose of feedback is to maintain and improve performance – it therefore should have both a positive intention and impact. It is vital that the whole feedback process, whether giving motivational feedback or developmental feedback, is conducted in a positive and constructive way.

EFFECTIVE MANAGEMENT DEVELOPMENT

When managers receive training in developing their competence and confidence in feedback skills, levels of engagement rise in their departments.

One of the key areas that can make a difference in raising engagement scores, therefore, is the amount of training and development that managers have to do their role. It is recommended that you review this and instigate plans to increase the amount of high-quality training that managers receive as part of an employee engagement strategy.

BP case study

BP, the oil and energy group, had no comprehensive development programme for the people who ran its retail outlets, supervised teams at oil refineries and chemical plants, or managed operations on drilling platforms. It didn't even have a common name for these key employees, who were known in different parts of the corporation as team leaders, supervisors or front-line managers.

In early 2000, BP's group chief executive set up a team of senior executives to rethink the organization's whole approach to learning and development. BP had just become the world's third largest oil company following a series of mergers and acquisitions. But the upheaval involved in creating a single entity out of British Petroleum, Amoco, Arco and several smaller firms had taken its toll on the workforce. Engagement surveys showed that front-line managers were especially dissatisfied, with many complaining about their supervisors or the absence of clear career paths. They often found it difficult to see how their individual decisions had contributed to the performance of the corporation as a whole. Nor was it always clear whether the skills and experience that a manager had gained in one part of the world could be transferred to another.

Addressing these needs was important to BP as 70–80 per cent of all BP employees reported to these managers. In order to improve first-line managers' skills and confidence a programme called 'First Line Leaders' was developed for all BP businesses around the world.

Run as a series of one-day workshops and attended by senior executives who spoke about their understanding of leadership and took questions from the floor, these events helped BP to develop its first-line managers' skills and give them the support they needed to do their jobs and deal with strategic challenges.

The performance of the leaders who have been through the programme since its launch in 2002 is consistently ranked above those who haven't taken part, both by their superiors and direct reports. The fact that senior BP executives deliver much of the content, alongside local and central HR and training professionals, has also helped to make the organization more capable and cohesive.

Key learning point

Providing management development training is an essential step in a programme of employee engagement.

Providing training to an organization's managers will make them feel that they are engaged and are given the support to do their job well. They in turn are more able to create the environment where their staff members feel engaged.

WHAT TYPE OF ENVIRONMENT DO YOU CREATE?

Use this self-assessment questionnaire to see what type of environment you create as a manager. You can also issue it to your team members and ask them to rate you against each of the questions. Then compare results. You could also use this with managers in your organization to create an awareness of their management style.

Thinking about yourself as a manager, rate how characteristic the behaviours listed below are of you. Use the following scoring system.

1 = Totally uncharacteristic, do this up to 10 per cent of the time
2 = Not characteristic, do this 30 per cent of the time
3 = Not very characteristic, do this 50 per cent of the time
4 = Somewhat characteristic, do this 70 per cent of the time
5 = Characteristic, do this 90 per cent of the time
6 = Totally characteristic, do this 100 per cent of the time.

Use Figure 9.5 to record your answers.

1. I praise others for a job well done.
2. I set others stretching goals.
3. I provide support for my team members when they need it.
4. I question others' approach to tasks and the impact of their actions.
5. I involve my team in decision making.
6. I tell my team members which areas they need to improve in.
7. I listen to others' points of view.
8. I set targets for individuals' development.
9. I encourage my team to do a good job.
10. I suggest alternative ways of doing things.
11. I ask my team members for their ideas.
12. I drive my team to constantly seek improvement.
13. I encourage others to work as a team.
14. My priority is for my team members to achieve targets.
15. I am approachable.
16. I expect high standards of others.

Score sheet

Question	Score	Question	Score
1		2	
3		4	
5		6	
7		8	
9		10	
11		12	
13		14	
15		16	
17		18	
19		20	
21		22	
23		24	
25		26	
27		28	
29		30	
	TOTAL this column: SUPPORT		TOTAL this column: CHALLENGE

Figure 9.5 Score sheet

17. I provide team members with guidance and advice.
18. I tackle poor performance.
19. I am interested in my team as people.
20. I state my expectations of my team members.
21. I build the confidence of others through praise.
22. I build team members' competence through pointing out gaps in their skills.
23. I value others' input.
24. I tell my team members if they are going off track.
25. I am considerate.
26. I like to raise the bar.
27. I make use of the strengths of my team members.
28. I am upfront about my team members' weaknesses.
29. I ask others how things should be done.
30. I tell others how things should be done.

Now map your scores on Figure 9.6. Plot where your two scores meet. Then turn to Figure 9.4 on page 202 to see which quadrant you fall in. Compare your scores with team members if you have asked them to assess you too. Prompts are provided below to help you capture your thoughts. Ask yourself:

▌ What is the type of work environment that you identified for yourself?

▌ What do other people identify as the work environment that you create?

▌ What are the differences in your scores compared to those filled in by others?

▌ Why might this be so?

▌ What is the potential impact of your scores on your team and their level of engagement?

▌ What do you need to do differently to create a more positive impact and high-performance culture?

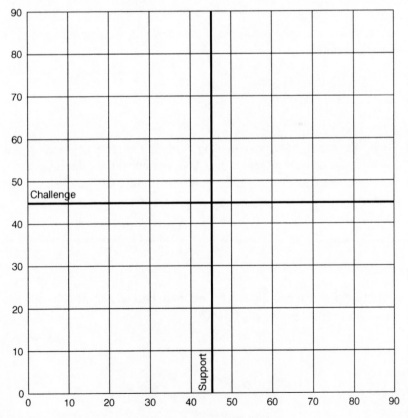

Figure 9.6 Support and challenge – score analysis

Checklist

What specific skills and abilities will you need to help you encourage employee engagement?

Consider your skills and abilities in terms of your:

- ability to read the political landscape;
- influencing skills;
- coaching skills;
- marketing skills.

What actions do you need to take to improve these?

How you will engender senior management support for employee engagement?

How will you create understanding that what leaders say and do and where they choose to spend their time will impact the success of any engagement initiative in your organization and ultimately impact your culture?

What support can you suggest to help them best align their behaviours to encourage employee engagement?

This chapter has looked at the roles of HR professionals, consultants or managers who want to act as an agent for change in their organization and at how they can achieve their task. It has also stressed the importance of the active support of the leadership team in acting as role models for employee engagement and how managers can create an environment that supports and encourages employee engagement. The final chapter addresses how to sustain a focus on employee engagement.

10

Sustaining a focus on employee engagement

Having looked at the WIFI model and how change agents, leaders and managers can create an environment that supports employee engagement, this final chapter looks at how you can sustain an employee engagement strategy.

ENGAGEMENT SCORES BEGINNING TO RISE

The optician retailer with whom we worked took specific action to create a better level of employee engagement. In the course of two years the organization undertook a number of initiatives. In the area of well-being it created better work–life and family-friendly policies. It also developed a new organizational vision, values and clear business goals that senior managers communicated via a series of roadshows, webcasts and on the intranet. In addition, the organization increased the amount of training that it provided managers and senior leaders, and also used the services of external coaches. In terms of fairness, a recognition scheme was started and a talent management programme has been created.

Organizational engagement scores began to rise. The next phase of the programme is to engender more involvement with staff. This is particularly important as the engagement survey showed that allowing people the opportunity to feed their views and opinions upwards is the single most important driver of engagement for the organization. Now the business is considering an innovations scheme plus fostering further cross-functional teamworking initiatives. It believes that the management and leadership development style is already changing across the organization due to the training it has provided.

One of the questions that the HR director is now tackling is how should the programme be sustained? There is talk in some quarters of the CEO who sponsored the programme moving on and the HR director is concerned that employee engagement still be a strategic objective and not just 'flavour of the month'.

CONTINUE MEASURING AND BENCHMARKING

I gave the HR director a number of pieces of advice, the first of which was to ensure that the business continued to measure employee engagement on a regular basis, develop action plans and communicate improvements. Secondly, I suggested that the organization benchmarked its key areas of development so that it could learn from best practice of other organizations.

However, there was other work that the HR director needed to influence to make sure that engagement was a continuing priority

IS EMPLOYEE ENGAGEMENT A STRATEGIC GOAL?

An issue to address if you would like employee engagement to have the importance it should, is whether this is a strategic goal for the organization. If not, what message is this sending the management team?

One business with which we worked publicly announced that it wanted to develop higher levels of customer and employee engagement. Yet when we looked at its strategic goals these centred purely on 'double-digit growth'. The key performance indicators were focused on sales and their employee benefits package again was entirely based on sales volume. There was nothing in their strategic objectives or measurement systems that spoke of the employee.

EMBEDDING EMPLOYEE ENGAGEMENT

My advice to the HR director was to ensure that employee engagement is embedded as a strategic goal and as a key indicator of business performance.

Following the maxim that 'what gets measured gets done', generally managers focus their attentions on the aspects of their role that will be measured. So if, for example, their key performance indicators are task- or sales-focused, this is where they will exert most of their attention. For managers to focus on employee engagement as a key priority, the most effective way of doing this is to make managers accountable for the engagement survey results of their staff.

Case studies

Sears

The starting point for culture change at Sears, for example, was the extensive research conducted via customer focus groups as well as employee focus groups looking at employee attitudes and behaviours. Drawing on this vast amount of interview and research data, the culture change team devised a series of performance measures which aggregated into an overall company measurement system, known as Sears Total Performance Indicators, or TPI. One-third of employee bonuses and incentives now derive from measures of employee engagement, one-third from customer measures and one-third from traditional financial measures.

B&Q

Likewise, after a period of rapid growth DIY retailer B&Q was faced with a period of spiralling cost of sale. At board level it was recognized that in order to face tougher market conditions the organization needed to increase the number of engaged employees that it had in the business. Working with research company Gallup, it now measures levels of employee engagement on a bi-annual basis. It combines these results with customer surveys, mystery shop reports and business performance measures. In addition it has increased the number of one-to-one meetings managers hold with employees.

The business has come up with the concept of the employee–customer–profit chain which shows that higher levels of engagement lead to greater customer satisfaction and better sales performance. Since beginning the survey and developing resulting action plans, business performance has improved. Managers are held individually responsible for the results of the engagement surveys in their areas.

Key learning points

▌ Integrate employee engagement into your measurement systems.

▌ Make managers accountable for engagement scores in their area.

Many corporations have adopted the 'balanced scorecard' as a management system that broadens the measurement of corporate health out beyond profit alone to embrace other factors such as customers and people satisfaction. Developed by Harvard Business School Professor Robert Kaplan and Davis Norton, President of management consultancy, Renaissance Worldwide, the approach is based on four key areas of measurement:

▌ learning and growth;

▌ internal business processes;

▌ customer service or satisfaction;

▌ financial performance.

A key feature of the balanced scorecard model is that it can be easily be customized. It is simple to change the dimensions on the scorecard to measures such as financial, processes, employee engagement and customers as its four areas of emphasis. Here are two organizations that have adopted this route.

Case studies

DSGi International

At DSGi International, the high street electrical retailer whose portfolio of brands include Currys, PC World and Dixons.co.uk, the results of the annual employee engagement survey for each unit are compared with their customer surveys and mystery shop results. Action plans have been developed to bring about improvements in each part of the business. For example, as a result of employee feedback, the reward scheme at Currys has changed from an individual to a team performance-based incentive. Employee engagement, customer satisfaction and financial results are the key elements of their balanced scorecard.

Norwich Union

Norwich Union has changed its senior managers' bonus scheme to link it to employee satisfaction.

The insurance company has restructured the bonuses of its top 120 UK senior management team so that 10 per cent is now linked to employee engagement and 10 per cent to customer satisfaction, with 30 per cent dependent on personal objectives and 50 per cent on financial performance. Prior to this, 70 per cent was based on financial performance and 30 per cent on personal objectives. The company are trying to stress that, before anything else, the role of a manager is to lead their people effectively.

For the past two-and-a-half years, Norwich Union has surveyed staff three times a year on managerial performance. All 1,000 managers received a report based on the data. The survey, which looks at 15 key criteria, was established by asking staff what they thought good leadership was. All managers are expected to score at least 60 per cent, with those who fall below being monitored and receiving support and training to improve.

Key learning points

▌ Ensure that employee engagement is one of the key elements of your business's balanced scorecard.

▌ Add employee engagement to all managers' performance objectives.

▌ Where possible, consider linking managers' remuneration to the improvement of employee engagement scores.

CONCLUSION

Evidence shows that engaging employees in the organization leads to long-term success. I hope that this book has provided you with advice and tips on how to increase levels of engagement among your employees using the WIFI principles of well-being, information, fairness and involvement. Here is a brief summary of the key points:

▌ Well-being encompasses feeling good about the organization and employees seeing that through its policies the organization is showing genuine care for them.

▌ Information is about having a clear vision of where the organization is going and what it wants to achieve and communicating this effectively. It is also about having clarity around organizational goals.

▌ Fairness should be seen in all aspects of the employee journey, from hiring the right people through to career and talent management.

▌ Involvement is about actively promoting and encouraging employees to give their views and opinions and empowering them to take decisions.

▌ By undertaking an employee engagement survey you can identify what factors are most important to your employees and where you can improve.

▌ Key to making improvements is the involvement and behaviours of business leaders and managers.

▌ Making improvements to the level of engagement is a long-term process that calls for change management skills and, above all, sustained management support.

References

Erickson, T and Grafton, L (2007) What It Means to Work Here, *Harvard Business Review*, March

Goleman, D (1996) *Emotional Intelligence: Why it can matter more than IQ*, Bloomsbury Publishing, New York

Heskett, J, Sasser, E and Schlesinger, L (1997) *The Service Profit Chain: How leading companies link profit and growth to loyalty, satisfaction and value*, Simon & Schuster, New York

Kaplan, R and Norton, D *The Balanced Scorecard: Translating Strategy into Action*, Harvard Business School Press, Boston, MA

Kotter, J (2002) *The Heart of Change*, Harvard Business School Press, Boston, MA

Leary-Joyce, J (2004) *Becoming an Employer of Choice*, Chartered Institute of Personnel and Development, London

Reichheld, F F (2001) *Loyalty Rules! How Today's Leaders Build Lasting Relationship*, Harvard Business School Press, Boston, MA

Spitzer, D R (1995) *Super Motivation: A blueprint for energising your organisation*, American Management Association, New York

Zohar, D and Marshall, I (2004) *Spiritual Capital: Wealth we can live by*, Bloomsbury Publishing, London

Research studies of employee engagement quoted in this book:

BlessingWhite: www.blessingwhite.com
Chartered Institute of Personnel and Development: www.cipd.co.uk
DDI: ddiworld.com
Hewitt Associates: www.hewitt.com
Institute of Employment Studies: www.employment-studies.co.uk
Sunday Times list of the top 100 companies to work for:
    www.bestcompanies.co.uk
Towers Perrin: www.towersperrin.com
Watson Wyatt: www.watsonwyatt.com

Further reading

Bayerlein, P and Gailey, R (2005) The six principles of performance communication, *Strategic HR Review*, **4** (4)

Bendapudi, N and Bendapudi, V (2005) Creating the living brand, *Harvard Business Review*, **83**, 5,

Brown, D (2004) Can employer branding deliver? *IDS Executive Compensation Review*, **279**

Causon, J (2004) The internal brand: successful cultural change and employee empowerment, *Journal of Change Management*, **4** (4)

Chartered Institute of Personnel and Development (CIPD) (2005) *Managing Change: The role of the psychological contract.* Change agenda, CIPD, London

CIPD (2005) *What is Employee Relations?* Change agenda, CIPD, London

CIPD (2006) *How Engaged are British Employees?* Survey report, CIPD, London

Cook, S (2007) *Customer Care Excellence*, Kogan Page, London

Cook, S, Macauley S and Coldicott H (2004) *Change Management Excellence*, Kogan Page, London

Conway N. and Briner, R (2005) *Understanding Psychological Contracts at Work: A critical evaluation of theory and research*, Oxford University Press, Oxford

Covey, S (1989) *The 7 Habits of Highly Effective People*, The Free Press, New York

Cully, M, Woodland, S and O'Reilly, A (1999) *Britain At Work: As depicted by the 1998 Workplace Employee Relations Survey*, Routledge, London

Daffy, C (2000) *Once a Customer, Always a Customer*, Oak Tree Press, Dublin

Dalby, C (2004) Developing an employer brand at Thomas Cook, *Strategic HR Review*, **3** (5)

Daniels, K (2006) *Employee Relations in an Organisational Context*, CIPD, London

Davenport, T O (1999) *Human Capital*, Jossey-Bass, San Francisco

Deery, S, Iverson, R D and Walsh J (2006) Toward a better understanding of psychological contract breach: a study of customer service employees, *Journal of Applied Psychology*, **91** (1)

Deery, S (2003) Engaging employees to live the brand: making your external brand a part of your internal culture, *Strategic HR Review*, **2** (6)

Deery, S (2004) Fair reward critical for employee engagement, *IDS Executive Compensation Review*, **283**

Deery, S (2005) Love me or lose me, *People Management*, **11** (23)

Emmott, M (2003) *HR survey: Where We Are, Where We're Heading*, Survey report, CIPD, London

Freiburg, K and Freiburg, J (1996) *NUTS! Southwest Airlines' Crazy Recipe for Business and Personal Success*, Orion Business, London

Gayeski, D M and Gorman, B (2005) HR's role in developing brand personality, *Strategic HR Review*, **4** (3)

Guest, D E and Conway, N (2004) *Employee Well-being and the Psychological Contract*, Research report, CIPD, London.

Hartley, V and Robey, D (2005) *Reporting on Human Capital Management*, IES Report 423

Hill, J (2006) Happy talk, *Personnel Today*, 30 May

Kersley, B, Alpin, C and Forth, J (2005) *Inside the Workplace: First findings from the 2004 Workplace Employment Relations Survey (WERS 2004)*, Economic and Social Research Council, London

Lawler, E. (1986) *High-involvement Management*, Jossey-Bass, San Francisco

Lawler, E (2003) *Treat People Right!*, John Wiley & Sons, New York

Leat, M. (2007) *Exploring Employee Relations*, 2nd edn, Butterworth Heinemann, Oxford

Marchington, M *et al* (2001) *Management Choice and Employee Voice*, Research report, CIPD, London

Marks, N (2006) Happiness is a serious business. In: *Reflections on Employee Engagement*, CIPD, Change agenda, London

Martin, G and Beaumont, P (2003) *Branding and People Management: What's in a name?* Research report, CIPD, London

Matthewman, J and Matignon, F (2005) *Human Capital Reporting: An internal perspective*. CIPD, London.

Merleverde, P, Bridoux, D and Vandamme, R (2001) *7 Steps to Emotional Intelligence*, Crown House, Carmarthen

Nelson, B and Swart, J (2003) *Understanding the People and Performance Link* Prentice Hall, London

Nordblom, C (2006) Involving middle managers in strategy at Volvo group, *Strategic Communication Management*, **10** (2)

Persaud, J (2003) Keep the faithful , *People Management*, **9** (12)

Pringle, H and Gordon, W (2001) *Brand Manners: How to Create the Self-Confident Organization to Live the Brand*, John Wiley & Sons, New York

Purcell, J *et al* (2003) *Understanding the People and Performance Link: Unlocking the black box*, Research report, CIPD, London

Quirke, B and Bloomfield R (2004) Developing a consistent planning approach, *Strategic Communication Management*, **8** (3)

Robertson, E (2005) Placing leaders at the heart of organizational communication, *Strategic Communication Management*, **9** (5)

Robinson, D, Perryman, S and Hayday, S (2004) *The Drivers of Employee Engagement*, Institute for Employment Studies, Brighton

Rogers, F (2003) Employer branding: fad or fact? *IRS Employment Review*, **778**

Scott, R W (2003) *Organizations: Rational, Natural and Open Systems*, Prentice Hall, New Jersey

Seybold, S (2001) *The Customer Revolution: How to thrive when your customers are in control*, Random House Business Books, New York

Stanier, M B (2001) Living the brand at Airtours Holidays, *Strategic Communication Management*, **5** (5)

Stevens, J (2005) *Unlocking the Black Box*, CIPD, London

Suff, R (2006) More than just a pretty face: building an employer brand, *IRS Employment Review*, **857**

Truss, C, Soane, E and Edwards, C (2006) *Working Life: Employee attitudes and engagement 2006*, Research report, CIPD, London

Ulrich, D and Brockbank, W (2005) *The HR value proposition*, Harvard Business School Press, Boston, MA.

Vita, E and Vernon, M (2007) Get engaged, *Management Today*, April

Wood, R and Tolley, H (2002) *Test Your Emotional Intelligence*, Kogan Page, London

Online resources

Center for Creative Leadership: www.ccl.org
The Conference Board: www.conference-board.org
Corporate Leadership Council: www.corporateleadershipcouncil.com
Gallup: www.gallup.com
Human Capital Institute: www.humancapitalinstitute.org
Human Performance Institute: www.corporateathlete.com
The Institute of Executive Development: www.execsight.org
SHRM: www.shrm.org

Index

NB: page numbers in *italic* indicate figures